iPad® Kickstart

Jay Kinghorn

New York   Chicago   San Francisco
Lisbon   London   Madrid   Mexico City
Milan   New Delhi   San Juan
Seoul   Singapore   Sydney   Toronto

The McGraw·Hill Companies

Cataloging-in-Publication Data is on file with the Library of Congress

McGraw-Hill books are available at special quantity discounts to use as premiums and sales promotions, or for use in corporate training programs. To contact a representative, please e-mail us at bulksales@mcgraw-hill.com.

iPad® Kickstart

Cover Image courtesy of Apple Inc.
Third Generation iPad product shot on the cover used by permission from Frederick Lieberath ©2012

1 2 3 4 5 6 7 8 9 0   DOC DOC   1 0 9 8 7 6 5 4 3 2

ISBN   978-0-07-180504-9
MHID   0-07-180504-4

SPONSORING EDITOR	**COPY EDITOR**	**ILLUSTRATION**
Megg Morin	Lisa McCoy	Cenveo Publisher Services and Lyssa Wald
EDITORIAL SUPERVISOR	**PROOFREADER**	
Janet Walden	Claire Splan	**ART DIRECTOR, COVER**
PROJECT MANAGER	**INDEXER**	Jeff Weeks
Vastavikta Sharma, Cenveo Publisher Services	Claire Splan	**COVER DESIGNER**
ACQUISITIONS COORDINATOR	**PRODUCTION SUPERVISOR**	Jeff Weeks
Stephanie Evans	James Kussow	
TECHNICAL EDITOR	**COMPOSITION**	
Janet Cloninger	Cenveo Publisher Services	

This book is dedicated to my wife Jessica and my son Remy. Jess, this book wouldn't have been possible without you. Thank you for all your hard work and support. Remy, you're growing up in a fascinating time and I know your love of books and learning will help you create a wonderful future.

About the Author

Jay Kinghorn (Salt Lake City, UT) is a thought-provoking author, provocative speaker, and Olympus Visionary photographer who helps companies adapt and innovate through technology training and creative services that helps them be agile and responsive in a rapidly changing business environment.

Kinghorn is a seasoned presenter and trainer who recently completed a multicity speaking tour for the American Society of Media Photographers on *Adaptation: Running a Successful Photo Business in Today's Era of Smartphones, Tablets, and Social Media*. Kinghorn frequently serves as technical director for National Geographic Photo Camps around the world, which brings teenagers from different cultures together to tell their stories visually using photography, multimedia, and the Web.

He is co-author, with Pulitzer Prize–winning photographer Jay Dickman, of *Perfect Digital Photography* (McGraw-Hill, 2009). Jay frequently blogs about visual literacy, photography, and the impact of technology and mobile publishing on society, commerce, and the arts at jaykinghorn.com and kinghornvisual.com.

Throughout his travels, the iPad has been Jay's constant companion, allowing him to stay productive, in touch, and entertained on the road and in the air.

About the Technical Editors

Janet Cloninger worked as a chemist and a programmer for many years before finding herself a work-at-home mom. Janet has written more than 2,000 articles and product reviews for The Gadgeteer, a well-respected site for reviews of gadgets and gear. Her love of gadgets came from her father, who never met anything he couldn't fix or improve. Janet lives in North Carolina with her husband, Butch, her daughter, Rachel, and their Shiba Inu, Teddy.

CONTENTS AT A GLANCE

CONTENTS

ACKNOWLEDGMENTS

Although my name is on the cover, this book is the result of a team of talented, hard-working collaborators. I would like to thank Jessica Kinghorn for being my partner in this endeavor, from brainstorming topic ideas and fleshing out the outline to being first-line editor, researcher, and sounding board for ideas. Thank you to Megg Morin and the team at McGraw-Hill: Stephanie Evans, Janet Walden, James Kussow, and Vastavikta Sharma. Janet Cloninger, thank you for bringing your expertise and passion for the iPad and ensuring technical accuracy in this book. Thanks to Susan and Steve Gleich, Pat Lehman and Dorothy Williams for providing early feedback on what they'd like to see in an iPad book. To Steve Heap for his insight on the best music apps and Sue Carroll at Apple for being a bridge between Apple and McGraw-Hill.

I would also like to thank all the app developers who've taken this wonderful device and transformed it into a versatile, powerful, and indispensable tool that will help usher in the next generation of computing and publishing.

INTRODUCTION

It seems rather fitting to be writing this introduction in a library—a repository of knowledge and learning. The Gutenberg press transformed the way we share and distribute knowledge, and has radically altered the course of human history. While I'm hesitant to make such grandiose statements about the iPad, it is clear that the iPad is part and parcel of a radical change in the way we access information. Rather than walk the immense floors of a library, we can browse virtual bookstores; read news commentary and insight online; watch TV shows; listen to music; and create, publish, and distribute our own work using the iPad and a host of apps. In only a few short years, the iPad has left an indelible mark on the way we think about and experience publishing, education, and entertainment.

I hope this book helps integrate the iPad into your daily routine and gives you a firm grasp on the ways it can change how you interact with the information in your life—from to-do reminders and business correspondence, to watching your favorite TV shows, to capturing and sharing the important moments.

To accomplish this, Chapters 1 and 2 provide the information you'll need to set up and configure your iPad, from the factory settings to new settings that reflect your needs and personality. Here you'll also find a step-by-step guide on transferring your apps, settings, and content from an iPad 1 or 2 to your third-generation iPad.

Chapter 3 helps you transfer your existing music, video, and app library to your iPad and customize your iPad's backup settings.

Chapters 4, 5, and 6 dive into the core apps you'll use most frequently on your iPad: Safari for web browsing; Mail for e-mail; and Contacts, Calendars, and Reminders for organizing your personal information.

Beginning in Chapter 7, I'll introduce you to the App Store, your gateway to the wider world of apps, and recommend five apps every iPad user should own. I'll also guide you on how best to transfer files between your iPad and your computer.

The iPad is a powerful, portable entertainment center, and in Chapter 8 I'll show you how to watch your favorite TV shows and movies, listen to your music library, or discover new songs and enjoy the wide variety of games available for the iPad.

Chapter 9 helps you discover the iBooks and Kindle apps, portals to fiction, nonfiction, and interactive e-books. I'll also show you how to catch up on the day's news and read commentary and insights from your favorite blogs using Really Simple Syndication (RSS) and social news-reader apps via the iPad.

In Chapter 10, unleash your creative genius using the iPad's built-in cameras to shoot photo and video; draw using the Multi-Touch screen; and create, edit, and share music.

In Chapter 11, I'll highlight the ways the iPad can impact every aspect of your life, from staying connected on your favorite social networks and exploring new recipes, to being productive in your business endeavors and using the iPad as an educational tool for the entire family.

Chapter 12 shows you how to use your Wi-Fi + Cellular iPad as a personal wireless hotspot; print documents to a variety of printers; and use AirPlay to stream movies, TV shows, and music to Apple TV and Wi-Fi-enabled sound systems.

The appendix helps you troubleshoot problems with your iPad and upgrade your iPad's operating system when updates are released.

I hope this book will serve as a trusted advisor by helping you explore the ways the iPad and its apps can be beneficial to your lifestyle, friendships, and productivity. Along the way, I hope you'll keep in touch. Please drop me a line at jay@kinghornvisual.com or a tweet @jaykinghorn if you find a great new app or have a profound iPad experience you want to share.

Conventions Used in This Book

Now You Know   The Now You Know sidebars provide deeper detail on a topic or specifics for accomplishing a task.

Tip   Tips help you make the most of your iPad by offering shortcuts or ways to streamline and super-charge your iPad experience.

Note   Notes aim to draw your attention to supplemental information, background steps, or additional hardware or software requirements.

Caution   Keep a sharp eye out for the Caution icon to help you steer clear of potential pitfalls or problems that may lie ahead.

1

Get Acquainted
with Your New iPad

Welcome to the third-generation iPad. In this chapter, I'll provide both new and experienced iPad users instructions to set up your iPad; get connected to the Internet; and understand the gestures, functions, and controls on your new device. For veteran iPad users, I will also demonstrate how to seamlessly migrate your apps, settings, and music libraries from your first- or second-generation iPad to your new third-generation iPad.

Your iPad Is Much More than a Little Computer

Because the iPad allows us to do many of the same things we do with our computers, like write e-mail, work with spreadsheets, or create corporate presentations, it is tempting to think of the iPad as a little computer. But this approach limits what the iPad can do for you. The iPad certainly can perform computer-like tasks, but other tasks play more to its strengths.

A better approach is to begin looking at the ways the iPad is uniquely suited to help us better organize our lives; reduce the stress associated with remembering tasks; or help us lead calmer, more fulfilling lives.

If we take a look at the built-in capabilities of the iPad—the touch screen, location awareness, an accelerometer and gyroscope, dual cameras, and a persistent Internet connection—a new paradigm emerges. An iPad is a tool that can integrate the online world with the physical world. Location information contained in our Wi-Fi and mobile Internet connections can tell us where in the world we are, and a quiver of mini-applications, or apps as they're more commonly called, can tell us what's around us—from historical landmarks to the nearest gas station or the best breakfast place within a half-mile.

The Difference Is in the Usability

As you begin to work with your iPad, consider the fundamental difference between using your touch screen to tap, swipe, pinch, and sweep through photos, videos, websites, or magazines as opposed to manipulating a mouse or track pad. The mouse requires coordination between two separate entities: your hand and the cursor on screen. In comparison, the touch screen is simple and direct, allowing you to simply touch the content you wish to control. The gestures used on the iPad—a pinch for zooming out, the opposite for zooming in, a swipe for sweeping between pages—are so simple even my toddler son understands the concept with minimal instruction.

Given that we've had 30 years to understand and integrate personal computers into our lives, it's natural to compare new devices, like the iPad, to our computers. As we enter a new era in computing, I encourage you to keep an open mind and use the iPad for its strengths. In this, and coming chapters, I aim to show you many ways you can put the iPad to work for you and use it for tasks that far exceed the capabilities of a little computer.

Set Up and Configure Your iPad

Before you can begin to explore this vast universe of apps, you first must set up and configure your iPad, get connected to the Internet, and configure a few basic preferences. This section walks you through the process, offering suggestions along the way to start your iPad experience on a high note.

What's In the Box?

Lifting the lid on your iPad's box feels like a grand unveiling. Your iPad sits front and center. Nestled beneath are a Universal Serial Bus (USB) cable, a power adapter, and a slender pamphlet with instructions on how to power up and begin using your iPad.

Go ahead and remove the clear protective film from the iPad so you'll have direct connection with the Multi-Touch screen. Beneath, you'll find a USB cable used to connect your iPad to your computer and to connect to the power adapter for charging your iPad in an electrical outlet. If you've purchased the Wi-Fi + Cellular model, your box will also contain a SIM eject tool that you'll use if you travel overseas and need to connect to a local mobile carrier. See Chapter 12 for specifics on why, when, and how to use this tool during travel.

Get Acquainted with Your iPad

Hold the iPad vertically, as shown in Figure 1-1, to see the buttons and features on the exterior of the iPad. In the center of the iPad's frame is the Home button, used to wake your iPad from sleep and exit out of an app you are using and back to the Home screen.

At the top of the frame is the front camera, which can be used as a still or video camera and is great for video calls with friends and family. See Chapter 6 for instructions on making video calls with FaceTime and Chapter 10 for using this camera to shoot photos and video.

Front camera

On/Off Sleep/Wake button

Silent switch

Volume up/down

Home screen

Home button

Cable connection

Figure 1-1 *Your iPad has only a few external controls used to power your iPad on or off, change volume, or return to the Home screen.*

Turn Your iPad On and Off

At the top of the iPad is the On/Off Sleep/Wake button. As you may have gathered from the long name, your iPad has two different "off" modes. You'll use the sleep mode most often, when you want your iPad to be ready to use but no longer want the screen active. To put your iPad in sleep mode, tap the On/Off Sleep/Wake button. To wake the iPad from sleep, tap either the On/Off Sleep/Wake button or the Home button.

Press and hold the On/Off Sleep/Wake button for three seconds to power your iPad off completely when it will be unused for an extended period of time. Swipe the red lock with your finger to complete the power-off procedure. You power back up by pressing and holding the On/Off Sleep/Wake button until an Apple logo appears indicating that your iPad is starting up.

Whenever you wake your iPad from sleep or power up from an extended hiatus, you'll be presented with the lock screen, which prevents your iPad from powering on with an accidental tap or a brush from other contents in your briefcase. Unlock the screen by sliding the lock with your finger from left to right.

Control the Volume of Speakers and Headphones

The Volume Up/Down rocker switch controls the volume of both the built-in speakers and headphones. Your iPad remembers the volume settings for your headphones and speakers independently so you won't be surprised by a loud blast of sound when you plug your headphones into the headphone jack on the top of the iPad.

Just above the Volume Up/Down button is the Silent/Screen rotation lock used to quickly mute the audio on your iPad.

Set Up Your iPad and Connect to the Internet

The initial setup process for the iPad is quick and straightforward, allowing you to get up and running quickly. In this section, I'll guide you through the setup steps and discuss which settings to choose to begin using your iPad immediately.

- **Welcome**   To unlock the iPad and get started, swipe the lock icon with your finger from left to right.

- **Language**   Select the default language you wish to use for your iPad's menus, settings, etc. English and Spanish are the two options on screen. If you'd prefer another language, tap the downward-pointing arrow to see other languages the iPad supports. Your language setting can always be changed later.

Tap the blue rightward-pointing arrow to continue.

- **Country or Region**   Select the country you'll use your iPad in most often so the iPad selects the appropriate dictionary for the dictation, auto-complete, and auto-correct features.

For this and subsequent screens within the setup process, you'll make a selection, then tap the blue Next button in the upper-right corner of the iPad to move to the next screen.

- **Location Services**   This allows the apps on your iPad to use your geographic location to customize information like maps, date and time, and search results displayed to you. I suggest enabling Location Services here.

 Chapter 2 shows you how to configure applications to allow or disallow use of your location so you can customize privacy settings to suit your needs.

- **Wi-Fi Network**   The iPad setup process requires an Internet connection to complete the activation process. If you have access to a Wi-Fi network, tap to select the network and, in the resulting dialog, enter the network's password using the iPad's onscreen keyboard. To access numbers and punctuation, press the .?123 key.

If you do not have access to a Wi-Fi network and own a Wi-Fi +
Cellular version of the iPad, tap the Use Cellular Connection
button to connect via a cellular data network.

If you do not have access to a Wi-Fi network and do not own a
Wi-Fi + Cellular version, connect your iPad to a computer and
complete your setup using iTunes. See "Set Up Your iPad Using
iTunes" for more information.

After you've established an Internet connection, Apple will
connect your iPad with their online activation service. This
process may take a few minutes to complete.

• **Set Up iPad**   If you have another iPad, you have the option to
use an existing iPad backup to copy your apps, settings, and
e-mail accounts to your new iPad. I'll cover the process in "Copy
Your Apps and Settings from Another iPad." Otherwise, select
Set Up As New iPad.

• **Apple ID**   Your Apple ID is a free account used to enable
synchronization of your iPad's settings with your computer,
iPhone, and Apple's cloud-based service, iCloud. If you have an
Apple ID and password, enter it in the fields provided;
otherwise, tap Create A Free Apple ID and follow the directions
to create a new Apple ID account.

 Chapter 3 explains how to set up and customize your synchronization,
backup, and storage options with iCloud.

• **Terms and Conditions**   Apple's Terms and Conditions document
covers your use of Apple's iCloud, Game Center, and other online
services and how your information may be used. Read the
document, then indicate your approval where specified to
continue the setup process.

- **Set Up iCloud** The iCloud service is used to synchronize your contacts, calendars, apps, and photos, and is integral to the iPad's seamless integration with your computer or Apple iPhone. On this screen, select Use iCloud to enable the service, and I'll show you how to customize the information iCloud syncs in Chapter 3.

- **iCloud Backup** Make sure you've backed up the data on your iPad to another location in case your iPad is lost, stolen, or damaged. You have the option to automatically back up your iPad to iCloud or to manually back up your iPad by connecting it to your computer. Select Back Up To iCloud unless you don't have regular access to a Wi-Fi connection. I'll discuss strategies for backing up to iCloud and iTunes in Chapter 3.

- **Find My iPad** I strongly recommend enabling Find My iPad, which allows you to use iCloud or the Find My iPad app on your iPhone to locate a lost or stolen iPad. With this service, you're also able to display a message on your iPad's screen, trigger an alarm, enable a four-digit passcode to deter thieves from accessing your private information, or even erase your iPad completely.

- **Dictation**   The iPad's Dictation feature allows you to speak to your iPad and have your speech translated to text. It is a great alternative to typing on the iPad's onscreen keyboard, and I encourage you to enable it here. I'll discuss the use of Dictation and provide tips for improving accuracy later in this chapter.

- **Diagnostics and Usage**   If you enable the Diagnostics and Usage function on your iPad, Apple will collect and transmit to their server anonymous information about your iPad's usage.

Congratulations! The setup process is complete and you're now ready to begin enjoying your iPad! Go ahead and jump to "Navigate Your iPad with a Tap, Swipe, and a Pinch" to begin working with your iPad.

Set Up Your iPad Using iTunes

If you do not have a Wi-Fi or cellular data connection available to activate your iPad, you'll need to connect your iPad to your computer using the USB cable and complete your setup using iTunes, the free software application for Mac and Windows from Apple that is used to manage your iPad's settings, apps, music, and video library. If your computer does not already have iTunes installed, download it from www.apple.com/itunes/download/ and install it on your computer.

Once installed, plug your iPad in to your computer and launch iTunes. The Set Up Your iPad screen will automatically appear once the iPad is detected by iTunes. Select Set Up As A New iPad unless you own another iPad and want your settings, including apps and app data like game scores, music playlists, and preferences, from your previous device to be copied to your new iPad.

Set Up Your iPad

In the next window, enter a name for your iPad and check the boxes corresponding to the iTunes content, like music, videos, and TV shows you'd like automatically copied to your iPad, then press Done to complete setup.

Set Up Your iPad

 I'll go into a lot more detail on customizing your synchronization options within iTunes in Chapter 3.

Copy Your Apps and Settings from Another iPad

If you already own a first- or second-generation iPad, you can seamlessly copy your apps, settings, Mail accounts, and iTunes library over to your new iPad.

 To ensure the most up-to-date information is copied to your new iPad, I recommend backing up your old iPad immediately prior to starting this process.

During the setup process, when you reach the Set Up iPad screen, tap the option corresponding to the backup method you've used in the past: either iCloud or iTunes. If you're unsure which backup method you've been using, use the Restore From iTunes Backup option if you routinely connect your iPad to your computer and use iTunes to manage your music and video libraries. If you have an iCloud account and work on the iPad wirelessly, select the Restore From iCloud Backup.

Set Up as New iPad	
Restore from iCloud Backup	✓
Restore from iTunes Backup	

Make your selection and press Next. Your iPad will switch to the lock screen and show "Restore In Progress." Do not attempt to use your iPad until the restoration is complete to ensure your content is fully copied to your new iPad. This process takes anywhere from 15 minutes to several hours depending on your connection (Wi-Fi versus USB) and the amount of content you have to synchronize.

When the process is complete, your iPad will be ready to use with your apps and content already installed. For security purposes, you will likely need to re-enter the passwords for your mail accounts and other secure data.

Navigate Your iPad with a Tap, Swipe, and a Pinch

Now that you've set up your iPad and are accustomed to the external buttons and controls, it's time to learn how to control your iPad using the language of the Multi-Touch screen—gestures.

- **Tap** The single tap acts like a single- or double-click of a computer mouse. A tap launches apps, places your text cursor on the page or in a web browser, and is used to make a selection or navigate for deeper functionality within an app.

- **Double-tap**   The double-tap is most often used for zooming in and out of documents, like the pages of a website or text document. Double-tapping a column of text zooms in to fill the screen with the width of the text. A second double-tap zooms out again. A hidden use of the double-tap found in most, but not all, apps is to tap near the top of the screen to quickly scroll to the top of a long page of text.

- **Swipe**   The swipe is one of the most versatile gestures on the iPad. A swipe with a single finger navigates between screens on the iPad, turns the pages of e-books, and scrolls through pages of content.

- **Drag**   Dragging is most often used to reposition items on screen, like moving a playing card from one stack to another when playing Solitaire or moving an e-mail from your Inbox to a specific folder.

- **Flick**   The flick is a quick pan or scroll. Frequently used for games, the velocity and angle of the flick can control a ball, a quick jump, or the sweep of a lethal weapon.

- **Pinch**   The pinch gesture with two fingers is used to increase or decrease the size of content on the screen or to zoom in for more detail. Move your thumb and index finger from close together to wide open to zoom closer to the content on the screen. Perform the opposite motion from wide open to closed fingers to zoom out.

- **Touch and hold**   Tap with one finger to insert a cursor for typing, or touch and hold to insert a magnifier to make it easier to place your cursor precisely. Read on for more information on typing and selecting text.

- **Shake**   A bit of a secret gesture, shaking or moving your iPad suddenly can be used to undo your most recent change, dodge a charging defender in a sports game, or roll the dice in a game of chance.

Get Started with Your iPad

Whenever you wake your iPad from sleep, you'll need to unlock it by swiping across the slider on the Auto-Lock screen. This will take you to the Home screen, Grand Central Station for your iPad explorations.

Your Home Screen

On the Home screen, you'll find your apps neatly arranged in an orderly grid. A series of dots below the app icons indicates the number of pages of apps contained on your iPad, and a lighter dot indicates your location within that order. Swipe with one finger to the right or left to access other pages of apps. Tap an app to launch it. Press the Home key to exit an app. There's no need to quit or exit an app before you press the Home button.

Rotate Your iPad for Easy Viewing

You'll typically hold your iPad in either a vertical, or portrait orientation, or horizontally in landscape mode, that mimics the width of a TV screen or computer monitor. Some games allow you to use your iPad like a controller—orienting the action around your rotation and movement of the iPad.

In most apps, you'll want to rotate the screen in whichever fashion is most comfortable for you. The contents on screen will usually rotate to accommodate your wishes. However, there are a few apps that only work in one orientation. If the content on the startup screen doesn't match the orientation of the iPad, that's a clue to turn the iPad to match the content.

Typing, Entering, and Formatting Text

Typing is an essential iPad skill. Because the iPad does not have an external keyboard, you'll want to master the onscreen keyboard for entering text in all your apps. In this section, I'll show you how to use the iPad to type, perform core text editing tasks like copying and pasting blocks of text, and correct inevitable spelling mistakes. And, if you're not content to use the iPad's onscreen keyboard, read on for how the Dictation app can translate your speech to text.

Type with the Onscreen Keyboard

To begin, tap an app like Notes to launch it and provide a place to practice your typing skills. Tap the location you wish to begin entering text, like you would with a computer mouse. The onscreen keyboard automatically appears along with a blinking cursor, just like on a computer. Type as you would on a computer keyboard, but note these differences:

- Numbers and commonly used characters like the @, &, or – symbols are found on the second keyboard screen, which is accessed by tapping the .?123 button.

- Less frequently used characters like #, }, or > are found on the third keyboard screen and are accessed by pressing the #+= key on the second keyboard.

- To hide the keyboard, press the keyboard key in the lower-right corner.

- To insert your cursor within a block of text, tap and hold your finger near the area you want to insert the cursor. A magnifier appears beneath your finger and allows you to select the insertion point with greater accuracy.

To quickly type a number or punctuation symbol from the iPad's second keyboard screen, tap and hold the .?123 button, then slide the same finger to the number you wish to enter. When you release your finger from the keyboard, the number or symbol will be entered and the keyboard will automatically return to the primary iPad keyboard layout.

Use the iPad's Built-in Intelligence to Avoid Mistakes

Apple knows that typing on the onscreen keyboard isn't as efficient as typing on a computer keyboard. Likewise, they know people can make typing mistakes, so they've built some "smarts" into the iPad to make typing more efficient and accurate.

As you type, the iPad's intelligent keyboard will attempt to auto-complete longer words or auto-correct words it thinks you are spelling incorrectly. Look for suggested words appearing immediately above or below your cursor, shaded with a different color than your current font. Accept the word by pressing the spacebar or dismiss the suggested

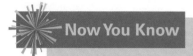

Now You Know   Use the Split Keyboard
for Faster Typing

The split keyboard makes typing with your thumbs (like typing a text
message) much faster than the hunt-and-peck method using your
index fingers. To split your onscreen keyboard, look for the four
ridged lines on the right side of the keyboard key. Touch and hold
the ridges, then drag the keyboard up off the bottom of the screen.
Once the keyboard splits, you can position the keyboard at a
comfortable location vertically on the screen.

To return to the normal keyboard layout, reverse your steps and
drag the keyboard back to the bottom of the screen.

word by continuing to type or tapping the small "x" to the right edge
of the suggested word's text block.

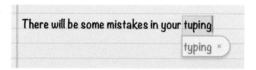

If you've reached the end of your sentence or block of text and see
misspelled words underlined in red, tap the word, and suggested
corrections appear in a bubble immediately above or below the
misspelled word. Tap the new selection to accept the change and
continue typing.

Here's another time-saving tip. Add a double-space at the end of
your sentence to automatically add a period and capitalize the first
character of the next word. These small time savers make typing a lot
more efficient.

The iPad remembers and learns from the words you accept and those you dismiss. This information is used to customize the dictionary and improve the accuracy of the intelligent keyboard.

The iPad's Hidden Text Features

There are additional features that make working with text more efficient. For example, double-tapping a word brings up the Edit menu with a set of contextual commands with additional actions.

Here are a few examples:

- In a typing environment (Mail, Books, Safari), the edit menu allows you to copy, select all, or define the currently selected word.

- When reading books in iBooks, the edit menu allows you to copy, define, highlight, or create a note. You can also perform a search within the book, on Wikipedia or on the Web, for the selected material.

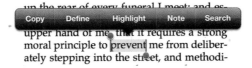

After you tap a word, you'll notice two vertical blue bars on either side of it. This allows you to select individual words or longer blocks of text. Use your finger to drag the first vertical bar to the front of your selection and the second vertical bar to the end of your selection. Then, tap the Copy or Cut (when available) command from the Edit menu to copy the text to the iPad's memory for use in another location or document.

ing the circulation. Whenever I find myself growing grim about the mouth; whenever

| Copy | Define | Highlight | Note | Search |

whenever I find myself involuntarily paus-
ing before coffin warehouses, and bringing
up the rear of every funeral I meet; and especially whenever my hypos get such an
upper hand of me, that it requires a strong
moral principle to prevent me from deliber-
ately stepping into the street, and methodi-
cally knocking people's hats off—then, I account it high time to get to sea as soon as I
can. This is my substitute for pistol and

When you're ready to paste the copied text, tap the insertion point and then tap Paste from the Edit menu. Or, select text you'd like to replace and then tap Paste to replace the existing text with pasted text.

Dictate Your Text to the iPad

Bypass typing entirely by using iPad's integrated Dictation. Open the app you wish to use (Messages, Mail, Safari, etc.) and tap the area you'd like text inserted. When the onscreen keyboard appears, click the microphone icon on the keyboard to activate the Dictation app. Once the microphone icon turns purple, begin speaking into the microphone located at the top of the iPad between the headphone jack and the On/ Off Wake/Sleep button.

 The Dictation app requires an Internet connection to function. If you do not have an Internet connection, the Dictation icon is removed from the keyboard.

When you finish speaking, tap the microphone icon a second time and the Dictation app will begin translating your spoken words into written text. Once the text is entered, verify that your words were translated successfully, then go ahead and deliver that e-mail message, start your web search, or complete your note, just as you would with any text you've typed on the keyboard.

Recharge Your Battery

When the battery runs out on your iPad, so does the fun. While you're using your iPad, keep an eye on the remaining battery charge by looking at the status bar, the thin black strip at the top of the screen.

Here, you'll see the percentage of the battery's charge remaining and, when your iPad is charging, the icon will change to the charging symbol.

.₁₁₁₁ Verizon 🛜	4:51 PM	41 % ▭

To recharge your iPad, plug the USB cable and power adapter directly into the wall. You can also connect the iPad to your computer using the USB cable, though some USB ports lack sufficient power to charge the iPad. As a result, you'll see the text "Not Charging" next to the battery icon in the status bar even though the iPad is connected to the computer. Most car chargers also lack the power to recharge an iPad successfully, as iPads require more power than your smart phone.

 If your iPad is extremely low on power, you may need to charge it for as long as 20 minutes before you'll have sufficient battery life to use your iPad.

Connect to the Internet

Your iPad is designed for consuming content, and increasingly, that content is downloaded, streamed, or accessed via the Internet. For that reason, the iPad makes it very easy to set up and manage your Internet connections.

Connect to a Wi-Fi Network

It is increasingly common to find Wi-Fi networks at coffee shops, airports, and other public places. Using a Wi-Fi network away from

 **Now You Know**   **Speak Your Punctuation to Improve Dictation Accuracy**

Verbally include commas and punctuation in your dictation. Although it sounds strange to say "I like pizza comma salad comma and key lime pie for dessert period," it greatly cuts down on the amount of editing you'll need to perform after you dictate.

The Difference Between Wi-Fi, 3G, and 4G Connections

All third-generation iPads can connect to a wireless or Wi-Fi Internet connection, like the kind you typically access at home, your office, or at a coffee shop or airport. These are the same connections you're probably accustomed to making with your desktop and laptop computer. The Wi-Fi + Cellular model can connect to cellular data networks, like the ones your smart phone uses for checking e-mail and mobile web browsing. These network connections are noted in the status bar with your mobile carrier and the type of cellular connection. Cellular networks are noted based on the generation of hardware used. For example, a third-generation tower is listed on your iPad as a 3G connection and fourth-generation as 4G. At the time of this writing, the fastest cellular connection type is LTE (Long-Term Evolution) and can provide faster upload and download speeds than most home-based broadband connections. The connection speed and type of cellular network available will vary by location and your carrier.

home will keep you connected and, if you have a Wi-Fi + Cellular model, will save on your monthly data allowance.

Tap the Settings app located on your Home screen and locate the Wi-Fi listing in the left column. Tap the Wi-Fi heading to show the Wi-Fi networks settings. At the top, you'll find an On/Off switch to enable or disable Wi-Fi connections and, when enabled, a list of Wi-Fi networks in the area. Next to the network's name, you'll see the Wi-Fi icon showing the strength of the network. Often, to the left of this icon you'll see a gray lock indicating the network is secured with a password that must be entered before you can join the network.

When you connect repeatedly to a network, say at home or work, your iPad will automatically reconnect to that network without prompting you to reenter your password.

Tap the network you wish to join and, if prompted, enter the network's password. Upon a successful connection, the network name will turn blue and show a check box next to the name. Tap your Home button to return to the Home screen.

✓ kinghornvisual 🔒 📶

On the left side of the status bar at the top of the screen, you'll see the wireless icon indicating you are connected to the Web using a Wi-Fi connection.

Connect to a Cellular Network (Wi-Fi + Cellular Models Only)

The Wi-Fi + Cellular model can connect to cellular data networks to provide a fast Internet connection when a Wi-Fi network isn't available. To connect to a cellular network for the first time, tap the Settings app on the Home screen and follow these steps.

1. Tap the Cellular Data heading to open the Cellular Data preferences.

2. Be sure the Cellular Data switch is set to "On."

3. Tap View Account to open your account preferences.

4. Fill out the account details form and select your data plan.

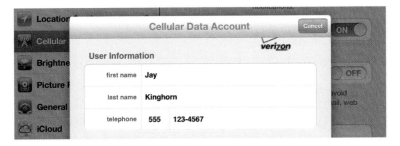

The plans offered will vary by service provider. Your iPad's hardware is specific to a cellular provider's data network and therefore you cannot switch service providers without purchasing a new iPad. In addition, your ability to modify or cancel your data plan is determined by your wireless carrier.

After you've completed your subscription with your wireless carrier, you'll receive a notification in your iPad that you're now able to use your cellular data connection in addition to Wi-Fi connections.

To do so, be sure your cellular data switch is set to On (as in step 2 of the procedure) and you are not connected to a Wi-Fi network. Your iPad will automatically connect to your cellular data network and indicate the connection type (3G, 4G, LTE) in the status bar.

 Because your cellular data plan bills you based on your Internet usage, it is advisable to use a Wi-Fi connection whenever possible to avoid surprise overage charges.

Use Airplane Mode to Go Offline

When you travel on an airplane, you'll need to disable your iPad's cellular connection for the duration of the flight, and your Wi-Fi connection for takeoff and landing. The Airplane Mode switch, located near the top of the Settings app, allows you to quickly disable the cellular connection for Wi-Fi + Cellular iPads. When Airplane Mode is on, an airplane logo will appear in the status bar. To disable Wi-Fi as well, tap the Wi-Fi heading and slide the Wi-Fi switch to "Off."

Protect Your iPad with AppleCare

AppleCare is an extended warranty for your iPad provided by Apple. The standard warranty included with every iPad covers one year of hardware coverage (defects in workmanship or excessive battery depletion) and 90 days of technical support.

The extended AppleCare+ warranty ($99 from Apple) boosts your hardware protection and technical support to two years and provides coverage for two accidental damage events, each subject to a $49 charge. Apple describes a damage event as "an operational or mechanical failure caused by an accident from handling that is the result of an unexpected and unintentional external event (e.g., drops and liquid contact)." As someone who travels frequently with my iPad and is always hustling to keep my iPad out of arm's reach of my toddler, this accidental damage coverage provides peace of mind.

To qualify for the extended warranty, you have to purchase AppleCare at the time of purchase or schedule a Genius Bar appointment at an Apple store to have your iPad inspected within 30 days of the original purchase before you can purchase the plan.

For more details, check out http://store.apple.com/us/product/S4689.

Get Help Directly from Apple

Working with a new device can be intimidating. If you purchase your iPad from an Apple retail store, you can have the staff set up and personalize your iPad, enable Find My iPad, and set up your Mail accounts before you leave the store.

Apple also offers free in-store classes to help you explore the world of apps or accomplish specific tasks with your iPad. These classes are a great supplement to this book. For more details visit www.apple.com/retail/personalsetup/.

2

Customize the iPad to Make It Yours

N ow that you've completed the setup process and taken a little
time to acquaint yourself with the iPad's features and
navigational structure, it's time to give your iPad a little personality,
to infuse it with your unique identity and make it *your* iPad.

Customize Your iPad's Appearance

In this section, I'll help you personalize the appearance of your iPad,
protect the screen, and select a custom photo to make your iPad
distinctive and unique.

Select an iPad Case

A cover or case is not only a means of identifying your iPad, but also a
protective measure to ensure the Retina display remains bright and
beautiful for a long time to come. I find a case makes it much easier to
hold and gives me confidence that I won't drop it. One of the simplest,
and most commonly used, iPad cases is the Smart Cover from Apple.
Magnets on the top and sides of the cover keep it in place. Once
secured, you can roll up the cover and flip it behind the iPad to serve as
an iPad stand.

There are thousands of other covers and cases that provide additional functionality, protection, and even productivity. The Logitech Ultrathin Keyboard Cover combines a protective case with a full keyboard for faster typing. Or, if fashion trumps productivity, you may consider a designer case from Louis Vuitton, Swarovski, or Hermes, which can set you back well over $1,000.

However you use your iPad, Macworld's editorial reviews are a great resource to help develop a short list of iPad cases to suit your needs, and budget. Learn more at www.macworld.com/products/tablets/accessories.html.

In a poetic sense, fingerprints on your screen affirm your iPad's unique identity. However, after a fevered brainstorming session over a plate of fries, that identity might need to be wiped clean and your iPad given a fresh start.

Apple recommends powering off the iPad completely, then wiping it down with a soft, slightly damp, lint-free cloth.

Control the Brightness of Your Screen

From your Home screen, tap the Settings app, then choose Brightness & Wallpaper to open the Brightness & Wallpaper preferences. You can use the Brightness slider near the top of the screen to brighten or dim your iPad's screen. Setting the screen at full brightness makes for arresting images, but will deplete your battery more quickly. Consider a dimmer setting for everyday work, and then crank it up when you're watching a movie or enjoying a slideshow of your favorite photos.

Immediately below the Brightness slider is the Auto-Brightness switch. When enabled, the iPad will automatically dim the screen to make for easier viewing in a darkened environment. I suggest leaving this on unless you find the changes in brightness distracting.

Customize Your Wallpaper and Lock Screen

Below the Brightness settings are two options for customizing the images, called wallpaper, displayed on the lock and Home screens on your iPad.

To change the wallpaper to an image of your choice, tap anywhere in the white box that shows the current lock and Home images on your iPad below the Wallpaper heading. Next, tap the Wallpaper heading to select one of Apple's preinstalled photos, or tap Camera Roll to choose one of your own photos. Users who have copied settings from another iPad may have additional options, including Photo Stream, which uses iCloud to synchronize photos between your iPhoto library and your iPad. If you've worked with your iPad before opening this book, you, too, may have additional options. Essentially, you're able to choose any photo from your iPad's photo albums at this stage.

In the next screen, tap a photo to select it and then choose Set Lock Screen, Set Home Screen, or Set Both to apply your photo to the appropriate screen(s). Afterward, the iPad will immediately return you to the photo category from which you made your selection. From there, you can start the process again if you'd prefer your Home and lock screens to have different background images.

Tailor Your iPad's General Settings

The General settings tab within the Settings app contains a wealth of information about your iPad and a collection of preferences to control everything from the sound played when you receive a new e-mail to the ability to restrict access to specific apps or types of content.

Review Your iPad's Vital Statistics

Let's begin with the trio of options at the top of the General preferences screen. Tap the About tab to discover a listing of your iPad's vital stats, including the number of songs in your music library and the amount of free space on your hard drive. Near the bottom of the list is the Diagnostics & Usage preferences I introduced you to in Chapter 1. This is the anonymous data Apple collects about the iPad functions, uses, and location. Should you wish to disable this feature, you can do so here. If you'd like to change this setting from the one you selected during setup, tap Diagnostics & Usage and choose Automatically Send or Don't Send. Tap the About button at the top of your screen to return to the About settings screen.

Tap the General button at the top of the screen to return to the General preferences.

A Sound for Every Action

The Sounds tab contains the controls for all the rings, tones, and chimes your iPad uses to herald the arrival of a phone call, an alarm for a calendar reminder, or an e-mail in your Inbox. At the top of the screen is a slider that controls the volume of the ringer and alert tones. Immediately below the slider is an option to connect the ringer and alert volume to the volume rocker on the side of the iPad, allowing you to change the volume of the alerts, even as they are sounding, without having to go to the Settings app to do so. Tap any of the alert headings, like Ringtones or Calendar Alerts, to hear a sample of the alert and select it for that feature.

The Lock Sounds option near the bottom of the Sounds preference screen controls whether or not the iPad emits a click when the iPad cover is opened or closed or the Auto-Lock is engaged or released. The second option, Keyboard Clicks, enables or disables the clicking sound of the keys on the keyboard. I prefer to leave both options off to make for a quieter iPad experience.

Tap the General heading to return to the top-level menu of settings contained in the General preferences panel.

Search Your iPad Using Spotlight Search

At times, it is a challenge to quickly find the address of an appointment you had a couple weeks ago, a phone number from within an e-mail, or an idea you jotted down in a note. Rather than spend time manually combing through the contents of your iPad, use the Spotlight Search feature to look for information—just like you would use a search engine to search for information online.

From your Home screen, swipe from left to right past your first page of apps to call up the Spotlight Search window. Begin typing the name of the item you're looking for, and Spotlight will scour the contents of your iPad to present you with the information you're looking for. Tap the listing to go directly to the information or app you searched for.

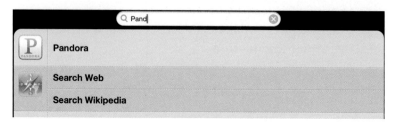

You can also bring up the Spotlight Search screen by pressing the main Home screen, the first page of apps on your iPad.

 You can use the Dictation feature to speak your search parameters and find content on your iPad.

If your Spotlight Search returns too many options, you may want to limit the types of information Spotlight displays. Within the General settings panel, tap the Spotlight Search heading to bring up the Spotlight Search preferences. Here, you'll see a listing of all the types of information Spotlight indexes, and searches, to provide answers to your queries.

To filter the types of information displayed in a Spotlight Search, tap the heading to remove the check mark for that type of data and eliminate it from your search results. Use the three horizontal "grabber" bars on the right side of each heading to prioritize the order Spotlight uses in presenting results. For example, if you'd like the contents of e-mail messages to appear near the top of the list, drag it just below Contacts in the list. These two options help make Spotlight more valuable at making the information on your iPad quite literally right at your fingertips.

Use Auto-Lock and Passcode to Protect the Contents of Your iPad

The next group of preferences you'll see serves to limit unintended use of your iPad, like preventing your iPad from powering on accidentally when you place it into a handbag or protecting your iPad from prying eyes using Passcode Lock.

The Auto-Lock feature helps minimize accidental use of your iPad by setting it to sleep when it isn't in use and protecting against an accidental awakening by requiring a user to swipe across the lock with their finger to access the contents of the iPad. Inside the General settings, tap Auto-Lock to specify the time period your iPad needs to be unused for Auto-Lock to engage.

If you leave your iPad around the house or office and don't want others to access its contents, engage the Passcode Lock to require users to enter a four-digit PIN number before the iPad can be used.

To engage Passcode Lock, click the Passcode Lock setting below the Auto-Lock preference in the General settings panel.

In the Passcode Lock settings panel, tap Turn Passcode On and enter a custom four-digit passcode that only you will know. After you enter the code the first time, you'll be prompted to reenter the code to confirm, and activate, your passcode.

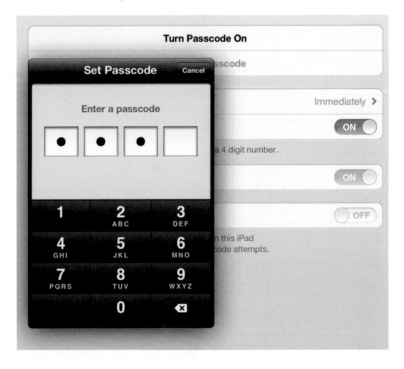

Now any users of your iPad will have to enter the correct passcode after the Auto-Lock screen.

If the wrong passcode is entered too many times, the iPad will be locked for increasing durations of time to deter a would-be snooper.

The remaining options on the Passcode Lock preference panel allow you to modify or boost the security of your iPad's contents:

- **Require Passcode** If you find the security of the passcode to be a helpful feature but think that reentering your passcode every time the iPad sits idle is tedious, you can specify a longer duration of time that must pass before the passcode must be entered again.

- **Simple Passcode** Disable Simple Passcode to change the passcode from a four-digit number to an alphanumeric (letters, numbers, and punctuation) password that is harder for would-be intruders to guess correctly.

- **Erase Data** Serious about security? Enable Erase Data to automatically erase the contents of your iPad after ten failed passcode attempts. If you choose this option, be sure you perform regular backups of your iPad.

To change or disable the passcode, click either Change Passcode or Turn Passcode Off. In both cases, you'll need to reenter the original passcode to make the change.

 If you forget your passcode, you'll need to restore your iPad using the computer you last used to sync it. This will delete any data added to your iPad since your last backup.

Restrict Access to Specific Content on Your iPad

If you don't want your child using your iPad to watch YouTube videos, or if you are a business owner using the iPad as a point-of-sale terminal and don't want your staff surfing the Web when they could be serving customers, you can restrict access to apps and specific types of content using the Restrictions setting.

From the main General Settings panel, tap Restrictions, then within the Restrictions preferences tap Enable Restrictions. You'll be prompted to enter and then confirm a four-digit Restrictions Passcode. This Restrictions Passcode is used to control access to the Restrictions panel, and only a user with the Restrictions Passcode can change the Restrictions Settings.

 For security purposes, your Restrictions Passcode should be separate from your regular passcode.

Once your Restrictions Passcode is enabled, use the on/off switches to control access to specific apps, Location Services, and multiplayer games, or to filter content for explicit language, movie, or TV ratings, and suggested age ranges for apps downloaded from the App Store.

Speed Up Your Use of the iPad

This section contains a series of minor tweaks to settings within the General preferences to make your iPad a little faster for common tasks you perform regularly:

- **iPad Cover Lock/Unlock**   This setting allows your Apple Smart Cover to put your iPad to sleep when the cover is closed or to wake it when the cover is opened, bypassing the Auto-Lock screen. This does not bypass Passcode Lock if it is enabled.

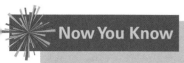

Create Shortcuts

Near the bottom of the Keyboard preferences you'll find a handy little service called Shortcuts that allows you to enter a short abbreviation for a longer word or commonly used phrase.

To create a new shortcut, tap the Add New Shortcut heading and, in the Phrase section, enter the text you'd like added. For the shortcut, enter an abbreviation for a longer phrase. Tap Save in the upper-right corner of the screen, and your shortcut is now active and ready to use in any app on your iPad. I like to use the shortcut to add a signature to my e-mails. Type your shortcut to display the longer text in a bubble adjacent to the text. Tap the spacebar to replace the shorter text with the phrase designated in the shortcut.

- **Use Side Switch To**   The Silent/Screen Rotation Lock switch on the side of your iPad, just above the volume controls (when the iPad is held vertically), can be used to lock the rotation of the iPad. To change the switch's function from a mute button to a rotation lock, tap the Lock Rotation heading in this setting.

- **Keyboard**   The Keyboard heading reveals a series of options to enable or disable Auto-Capitalization, Auto-Correction, Check Spelling, and other features.

Get Advised with Notification Center and Alerts

When Apple introduced iOS 5, the operating system running on your iPad, one of the key new features was the Notification Center—a central location to aggregate all the timely information your iPad collects for you. Think of the Notification Center as the dashboard to your busy life.

With a quick glance you can see who's commented on your Facebook posts, check your calendar for the day's events, or learn that your flight to San Francisco is delayed by 20 minutes. To ensure the dashboard is as useful to you as possible, I'll introduce you to Notification Center, then I'll guide you on customizing the style and display of notifications you receive from the applications and services you use most.

Access and Configure Notification Center

The Notification Center can be accessed from any app or screen on your iPad by dragging your finger downward from the top of the screen. This gesture reveals a column of information culled from the apps you allow to appear within the Notification Center. Close it by dragging your finger from the bottom of the Notification Center to the top of the screen.

To prevent Notification Center from becoming cluttered, you'll want to customize which of your apps are allowed to post to it. As your app library grows, you'll probably want to return periodically to your settings to ensure you're still seeing the notifications that are most important to you.

To access the Notifications preferences, tap the Notifications heading near the top of the left column in the Settings app. You'll see the information on screen divided into three categories:

- **Sort Apps**   Allows you to specify whether notifications are grouped by app or displayed chronologically

- **In Notification Center**   The apps allowed to post in your Notification Center

- **Not In Notification Center**   Apps excluded from Notification Center

Tap the heading for any of the apps listed to bring up that app's Messages preferences. At the top of the screen, you'll find a switch to include (On) or exclude (Off) the app from the Notification Center.

Now You Know   Prioritize Notifications

Within the Notifications preferences, you can prioritize the order apps appear in the Notification Center by tapping the Edit button in the upper-right corner of the screen. A gripper bar appears on the right side of each app's heading, which allows you to drag apps into the order you'd like them presented to you within Notification Center. You can even drag apps in and out of Notification Center.

Immediately below the switch you can specify whether you want the most recent 1, 5, 10, or 20 notifications from the app to display in the Notification Center.

Manage Alerts and Interruptions

The Notification Center isn't the only way the apps on your iPad communicate with you. When you launch an app for the first time, you'll be prompted to choose whether or not to allow the new app to send you notifications. Choosing Allow will permit the app to deliver notifications based on the app's default preference.

The iPad uses three different ways to get your attention, with important information, banners, and alerts:

- **Banner**   A banner notification briefly appears at the top of the screen and then disappears after a few seconds. Banners are ideal for keeping you in the loop without interrupting your work or play.

- **Alert**   An alert badge appears in the center of the screen and requires you to perform an action to dismiss the badge. Typically, alerts are reserved for important information within an app, but they can also be used to grab your attention from the Home screen when the iPad is not in use.

- **Badge App Icon**   The least obtrusive of the notification types is the badge icon, a simple red circle with a white number indicating the number of pending notifications that appears on the corner of the app's icon on the Home screen.

Like most everything else on the iPad, the alerts you receive, and how they're presented to you, can be customized from within the Settings app.

A few of the core apps in the App Store do not provide settings for adjusting notifications.

Tap the Notifications heading, then tap an app to bring up the app's notification and alert preferences. In the Alert Style heading, tap to select the type of alert you would like this app to provide to you.

Some apps, like Messages, allow you to specify whether or not a preview of the message is shown within the alert and whether the alert is repeated.

My preference for handling notifications is to enable Notification Center and banner notifications for information-based apps that I use most often (Calendar, Facebook, Twitter, Messages, Travel Apps, to-do lists, etc.) and set the remaining apps to either a banner or none. This minimizes the number of times I'm interrupted while working on my iPad and allows me to be in control of my alerts and notifications.

What Are Location Services?

One of the greatest strengths of a mobile device like the iPad is the ability to display information relevant to your physical location. With the right apps installed, your iPad can display reviews of restaurants within walking distance, directions to take public transportation from your hotel to a museum, or a listing of friends from your social network who happen to be nearby. In addition, a variety of web-based services like Groupon Now! are emerging to provide discounts or advertisements to customers in close proximity to certain retail locations.

To access these streams of information, your iPad needs to relay the location of your iPad to the appropriate app. It determines your location using information from Wi-Fi and cellular networks, then feeds your location to the apps via Location Services. However, sharing your location with the world can have its drawbacks. That's why the iPad gives you control over which apps have access to your location. This affords you control over your privacy while still being able to take advantage of the benefits of geolocated services.

Use Location Services to Protect Your Privacy

During the initial setup of your iPad, you were asked if you wanted to enable Location Services. I recommended selecting Yes so you can take advantage of all the great benefits location provides to your iPad experience. In addition, by configuring your Location Services preferences here, instead of during setup, you can determine which apps have access to your location, thus providing far more control than the simple Yes/No option given during setup.

Access the Location Services preferences, like the other preferences we've discussed thus far, within the Settings app. Tap the Location Services heading to bring up the Location Services preference panel. Here, you'll see a switch at the top of the screen to enable or disable Location Services entirely, along with on/off switches for each of the apps you have installed that are capable of using location information.

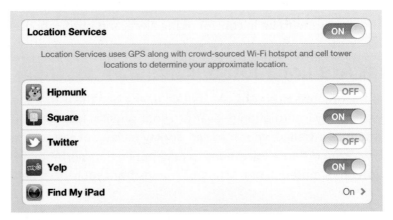

Some apps require Location Services to be enabled in order to operate. You'll see an alert appear when launching an app that requires Location Services if you've disabled Location Services entirely or revoked permissions for that app.

Ultimately, it is important to be aware of how information is continuously gathered over the Internet, particularly as more of our devices (phones, cars, even household thermostats) are connected 24/7 to the Internet. I appreciate that Apple provides us with the tools to control the flow of this information from our devices.

If this discussion has piqued your curiosity as to which apps are tracking your whereabouts, look for the color-coded compass arrows located next to the apps listing on the Location Services preference page. A purple arrow indicates the app is using your location right now. Gray indicates the app has used your location within the last 30 days, and a purple outlined icon (not the solid ones listed earlier) indicates the use of a geofence, a tool used to trigger an action like a message or a killer restaurant deal when your iPad physically enters a specific geographic location.

How Should I Configure Location Services?

My recommendation is to enable Location Services for the apps that use your location to provide a direct benefit to you. As an example, when I travel I often use the Yelp app to lead me to a great meal without having to travel far from my hotel.

A second category of apps uses location as a shortcut for the kind of information you commonly use the app for. An example is the Weather Channel app that uses your location to show the weather in your area. You could manually enter that information, but Location Services saves you a step. I tend to allow Location Services on a case-by-case basis for this kind of service. If I use the app frequently and I find the location shortcut useful, I keep it enabled. Otherwise, I shut it off.

Additional Settings Preferences

As you can see, there are far more preferences available to configure than we've covered in this chapter. Many of those apply to specific apps like Mail, iCloud, or Safari that we'll cover in later chapters. Other preferences are specific to a single app like Skype. Rather than go through these, I'll encourage you to look through these preferences on your own to discover more ways you can customize the features, settings, and services of your iPad.

3

Use iCloud and iTunes to Sync and Back Up Your iPad

Your iPad is not an island. Or, at least it *shouldn't* be. Connecting your iPad with your iTunes library and iCloud, a synchronization and storage service, amplifies your ability to integrate the content you enjoy on your iPad with the rest of your life. This way, you have the flexibility to do things like control which songs from your iTunes library are copied to your iPad or schedule a meeting on your iPad's calendar and have a reminder appear on your iPhone ten minutes before the meeting begins.

iTunes and iCloud are the key elements to this organizational magic. In this chapter I'll introduce you to each tool and outline the roles they play in coordinating your iPad with your other devices. Then, I'll help you synchronize your photos, videos, and apps using iTunes, and help you enable iCloud to sync your important data like calendars and your address book.

iCloud, iTunes, Your iPad, and You

Apple's iTunes and iCloud are complementary services that make the process of synchronizing your data and managing the content on your iPad automatic and seamless. iTunes is a free desktop application that originally gained popularity as a tool for organizing your personal music library and synchronizing your songs to your iPod. Over time,

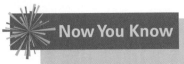

Now You Know   What About MobileMe?

Apple's MobileMe, the predecessor to iCloud, has been discontinued and all MobileMe services will be terminated as of June 30, 2012. All MobileMe subscribers will need to migrate their accounts to iCloud and use its newer, and significantly improved, features. For more details, or to upgrade your MobileMe account to iCloud, visit www.me.com.

it has grown into a media manager that is tightly integrated with the online iTunes Store for purchasing music, renting movies and TV shows, subscribing to free podcasts, or downloading apps. You connect your iPad with iTunes by plugging your iPad into your computer using the USB cable.

iCloud is a web-based service that stores an online copy of your calendars, address book contacts, e-mail, and apps. As you use your iPad, iPhone, and computer, iCloud aggregates this information and updates all of your devices, ensuring everyone has the most up-to-date information. You connect your iPad to iCloud wirelessly using Wi-Fi.

Many of iTunes and iCloud's core functions, like synchronization and storage, overlap. Therefore, it is possible to use your iPad successfully using just one of these tools. However, I find it is most effective to select the best attributes of each service and use them in tandem. This way, you can take advantage of the immediacy and convenience of synchronizing time-sensitive information like Calendar appointments with iCloud and use the storage capacity of your computer and fast transfer speeds of USB to manage your photo, video, and music libraries through iTunes.

Use iTunes to Manage Your Music, Photos, and Videos

You've probably downloaded most of your favorite music to your computer. And many of you already have iTunes installed on your computer and use it to sync with an iPad, iPhone, or iPod. Because iTunes is a familiar application for many people, it serves as a logical place for starting to transfer your existing music and video libraries to your iPad.

What Type of Computer Do I Need?

To connect your iPad with the most current version of iTunes, you'll need to be sure your Macintosh or Windows operating system meets the system requirements listed here:

- A USB 2.0 port
- Mac OS X version 10.5.8 or later

or

- Windows 7, Windows Vista, or Windows XP Home or Professional with Service Pack 3 or later
- iTunes 10.6 or later

Update to the Current Version of iTunes

If you don't already have iTunes installed on your computer, type **www. itunes.com** into your computer's web browser and download the free application for either Mac or Windows operating systems.

If you have a version of iTunes installed, it is wise to verify that you have the most up-to-date version, so you can benefit from any changes iTunes has recently made and ensure compatibility with your iPad.

To check for updates on Macintosh:

1. Launch iTunes.
2. Under the iTunes menu at the top of the screen, select Check For Updates.

To check for updates on Windows:

1. Launch iTunes.
2. Click the Help menu and select Check For Updates.

If a newer version of iTunes is available, follow the simple directions to install the software.

An iTunes Primer

On the iPad and your computer, iTunes is your entertainment center and media manager. It allows you to store, organize, and play your personal music and video collection; explore and purchase new music, electronic books, and TV shows; rent movies; and delve into the world of podcasts and episodic audio and video shows covering every topic imaginable.

Because iTunes is multifaceted and works differently on your computer than on your iPad, I wanted to take a moment to clarify those differences, so you're clear on the role each plays when you want to sync your content or later enjoy it on your iPad.

On your computer, iTunes is used to play music, videos, movies, TV shows, and podcasts. This content may have been purchased through the online iTunes Store or acquired through other means—copied from your CD collection or purchased from another online music retailer. iTunes on your desktop also acts as a portal to the iTunes Store, where you can purchase and download new content. iTunes also serves as a synchronization and content management tool for your iPad and other Apple devices, which is the focus of this section.

Unlike on your computer, where you can listen to and watch media through iTunes, on the iPad these functions are split into several different apps, including Music, Videos, iBooks, and the App Store.

I'll show you how to use the iTunes and associated iPad apps in Chapter 8. For now, I'll focus on showing you how to get your existing content onto your iPad and set up your synchronization processes.

Synchronize Your iPad with iTunes

Connect your iPad to your computer using the USB cable and launch the iTunes application if it doesn't launch automatically. If this is the first time you've connected your iPad to your computer, you will receive an alert dialog asking if it is okay to sync your iPad to this computer. Provided this is the computer you'll be using to store and manage your music library, select OK. Your iPad can only be synchronized with one computer at a time, so if you have more than one computer, you'll want to sync with the computer you use to store your music and video libraries.

Once the connection between your iPad and the computer is made, iTunes will automatically begin to sync the apps, music, and settings with any content you have stored in iTunes on your computer. This is a two-way synchronization to ensure your iPad and your computer each have a complete and up-to-date copy of everything on your iPad and in your iTunes library.

To view or modify your iPad's sync options within iTunes, click your iPad's name beneath the Devices heading in the left column of the iTunes window. The iPad sync options are segmented by content type into ten separate headings located at the top of the iPad sync window.

On the Summary page of your iPad's listing within iTunes you'll find a summary of key statistics contained within four separate headings:

- **iPad**   The iPad heading displays your iPad's name, storage capacity, serial number, and iOS software version.

- **Version**   This heading contains two important buttons. The first button, Update, checks for or installs updates to your iOS operating system. The second button, Restore, allows you to restore your iPad from an earlier backup copy in the unlikely event you begin having problems with your iPad.

- **Backup**   The Backup tab allows you to choose between backing up your iPad to iTunes or to iCloud. iTunes backups are more comprehensive than iCloud backups and, for that reason,

I recommend backing up to iTunes instead of iCloud if you will connect your iPad to your computer at least weekly. I'll go more into depth on iCloud versus iTunes backups later in this chapter.

Backup

○ Back up to iCloud
◉ Back up to this computer
　☐ Encrypt local backup [Change Password...]
Last backed up to this computer: 5/3/12 9:33 AM

Located in the Backup box, the Encrypt Local Backup option adds password protection to your iPad backups stored on your computer. This step adds a measure of security for your personal data and speeds up the process of restoring from a backup, as you won't have to reenter passwords for your accounts.

- **Options**   The Options panel has two preferences worth noting. The top check box will automatically launch the iTunes app when you connect to your iPad. This ensures your iPad will be backed up when you connect to your computer, provided you're using iTunes as your backup method.

Use the Sync With This iPad Over The Wi-Fi option to synchronize your iPad with iTunes via Wi-Fi instead of USB. The sync may take a long time, so Apple requires you to plug your iPad into a power source before beginning the sync so it does not run out of power during the process.

At the bottom of the iTunes window is a summary of your iPad's hard drive usage and remaining space available. This is helpful for managing the content on your iPad and ensuring you have sufficient space for all the music, videos, games, and apps you want to use on your iPad.

Control iTunes Synchronization

It is quite likely that you'll want to transfer a subset of your entire iTunes library to your iPad. This can be a space-saving tactic or beneficial if you want to store your favorite songs, unwatched TV shows, or unread books on your iPad, keeping a complete collection on your computer. iTunes makes it easy to control the content synchronized between your computer and iPad using the remaining nine headings at the top of the iTunes synchronization window.

Because some of these sections will be more relevant to you once you've spent more time working with and adding content and apps to your iPad, I've subdivided these menus into separate headings for you to return to quickly when the need arises.

Info

The Info window can be used for synchronizing your contacts and calendars, but I don't recommend using iTunes to do so. Instead, I suggest copying this information via iCloud, which gives you near-instant updates across all your devices. These options are disabled by default.

 Synchronizing your information with iTunes and iCloud may cause duplicate information to appear in your calendar and contacts list.

Apps

The Apps tab is used for two important tasks. First, it allows you to control which apps you sync with your iPad. This is particularly important if you have an iPhone and an iPad, as you may not want all your iPhone-specific apps to appear on your iPad.

To manage which apps are synced to your iPad, scroll through the Sync Apps column on the left side of the screen. Uncheck the box to the left of any app's icon to remove it from the list of synchronized items. This will remove the app and delete any app-specific data (like files, playlists, or preferences) from your iPad.

From the pull-down menu below the Sync Apps heading, you can opt to sort the apps by kind, which allows you to group all the iPhone– and iPod touch–specific apps to remove them quickly.

Within this window, you're also able to organize the apps on your iPad and group them into folders or place them in a custom order on your Home screens. I'll show you how to do this within iTunes on your computer and on your iPad in Chapter 7.

The second use of the Apps tab is to transfer files between your computer and apps designed to work with and save individual files, like text-editing apps. I'll cover ways of transferring files between your iPad and your computer in Chapter 7, when you'll start working with apps on your iPad.

Music

Here you have the option to sync the music in your iTunes library with your iPad. For many avid music listeners, your iTunes library may well exceed the storage capacity of your iPad. If you're among this group, you'll need to copy a subset of your music library to the iPad by synchronizing a hand-selected playlist of your favorite tunes or a smart playlist to automatically pull your most listened to, highest rated, or most recently added tracks to your iPad.

 To view the total size of your iTunes music library, click the Music tab under the Library heading in the upper-left corner of your iTunes window. The total size of your music library will be displayed at the bottom of your screen.

6893 items, 21.2 days, 41.70 GB

To sync your entire iTunes music library to your iPad:

1. Select the Sync Music check box to enable iTunes to sync music with your iPad.

2. Select the Entire Music Library radio button from within the Sync Music heading.

3. In the lower-right corner of the iTunes window, click the Apply button to confirm your changes, and then click Sync to synchronize your iTunes music library with your iPad.

To copy a subset of your iTunes music library to your iPad:

1. Select the Sync Music check box to enable iTunes to sync music with your iPad.

2. Under the Sync Music heading, choose the Selected Playlists, Artists, Albums, And Genres radio button. You have three options here: Include Music Videos, Include Voice Memos, and Automatically Fill Free Space With Songs. I don't recommend filling the free space, as it could prevent you from downloading new apps, creating or adding documents, or purchasing new music from your iPad.

3. Below the Sync Music heading are four additional headings used for manually selecting the music tracks, genres, albums, or artists you'd like copied to your iPad.

4. In the lower-right corner of the iTunes window, click the Apply button to confirm your changes, and then click Sync to synchronize your iTunes music library to your iPad.

Copy Your Favorite Songs to Your iPad with a Smart Playlist

Using a Smart Playlist within the desktop version of iTunes, you can automatically pull songs from your music collection based on a predefined set of criteria. Here, I'll show you how to create a Smart Playlist to pull only the freshest and most-listened to songs on your iPad.

1. In iTunes, select File | New Smart Playlist.

   In the Smart Playlist window, you're able to define the criteria used to add songs to the playlist. The criteria can be modified by clicking the heading and selecting a new option from the pull-down menu.

2. In the first column (currently labeled Artist), select Plays. In the second column select Is Greater Than and in the text field enter a minimum number of plays a song must have to make it into your Smart Playlist. You'll need to experiment with this number a bit to limit the playlist sufficiently to fit on your iPad. For my playlist, I entered 30 as the minimum number of plays.

3. Click the plus sign (+) on the right side of the box to add a second set of criteria from the playlist. A checked box called Match will appear at the top left of the dialog box. The box should remain checked. Then, change the pull-down menu to the right of Match from All to Any.

4. In the second row, first column, choose Date Added from the pull-down menu. In the second row, second column, choose In The Last from the pull-down menu, and in the text field enter **60** days. This adds to your playlist any songs added within the last 60 days, which likely will not have received enough plays to meet the first criteria.

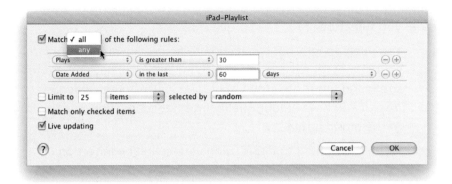

5. Click OK to create your Smart Playlist, and then click the heading of your newly created "untitled playlist" and give it the title of **iPad-playlist**.

6. Click the iPad heading from the Devices heading in the left column of iTunes and return to the Music heading.

7. In the Playlists heading, select iPad-playlist from the list.

8. In the lower-right corner of the iTunes window, click the Apply button to confirm your changes, and then click Sync to synchronize your iTunes music library with your iPad.

What Is iTunes Match? Is It Right for Me?

This new service from Apple allows you to stream your music collection of up to 25,000 songs on up to ten Apple devices, including your iPad, iPhone, iPod touch, your computer, and Apple TV. When you subscribe to iTunes Match, iTunes scans your music library to find matches with music stored on iTunes. Any songs you have in your collection that aren't part of iTunes (your nephew's fledgling punk band, for example) are uploaded to your iCloud account where they can be streamed as part of your iTunes library. For $25 a year, the promise of having your entire music library with you, wherever you are, certainly sounds promising. In practice, however, there are a few gotchas to be aware of before you subscribe:

- You need an Internet connection to access the music stored in your iTunes Match account, which means you'll have a hard time streaming music on airplanes or long walks in the wilderness. Also, if you have a poor-quality Internet connection, the quality of the music suffers.

- If you're listening to music using your cellular connection on a Wi-Fi + 4G model, you'll need to pay more attention to your data usage. Your streamed music counts against your monthly data plan, and you'll want to adjust your data plan accordingly to avoid overages.

iTunes Match is an ideal companion to a hand-picked selection of your favorite tracks that you've synchronized to your iPad. This way, you have the songs you listen to most often always at the ready. And when you get a craving to hear "Sweet Home Alabama," a song you haven't listened to in two years, it will be there to satisfy that craving.

Movies

The Movies section within iTunes contains any movies you've created, video files you've added to iTunes, and movies rented through the iTunes Store. More so than any other type of content, movies, due to their large file size, have the potential to hog storage space on your iPad. For this reason, you'll want to pay close attention to which movies you decide to store.

At the top of the window, the Sync Movies check box allows you to enable or disable movie synchronization. Visible just below the heading, the Automatically Include...Movies Along With Selected Movies check box acts like a Smart Playlist to copy only the movies that meet specific criteria. For example, you may want to copy only movies you haven't yet watched. The pull-down menu in the center of the Automatically Include... sentence allows you to choose the criteria for copying movies to your iPad. Uncheck this feature if you'd like to manually select movies for your iPad library.

☑ Sync Movies   23 movies

   ☑ Automatically include | all unwatched   ⬍ | movies along with selected movies

When the Automatically Include… option is unchecked, you can use the Movies heading to peruse your movie library and check the boxes next to the movies you'd like copied to your iPad. When doing so, keep an eye on the iPad storage graph at the bottom of the window, as it will dynamically update based on your selection so you can be sure you have enough space to copy all your selected movies.

When you're finished making your selections, click the Apply button in the lower-right corner to apply your changes and begin synchronizing your iPad with iTunes.

Renting Movies from the iTunes Store

The iTunes Store is a great resource for renting and watching movies wherever you and your iPad are. You can rent movies on either your iPad or iTunes and transfer your rented movies between devices, though a movie can only be watched on one device at a time. Your rental period allows you 30 days to begin watching the movie and 24 hours to finish watching the movie once it starts.

To transfer a movie rented using iTunes on your computer to your iPad:

1. Select your iPad from the Devices heading on the left side of the iTunes application.When you've rented a movie, a Rented Movies tab appears at the top of the Movies heading. You'll see a listing of your rented movies, along with the time remaining in your rental.

2. Adjacent to the rented movie, a Move button allows you to move the rental from your computer to your iPad and vice-versa.

Rented Movies   On "Jay Kinghorn's iPad"

The Descendants
115 minutes
1.53 GB
Expires in 29 days and 22 hours
R   Move

3. Click Move to send the movie to another device, and then click the Apply button in the lower-right corner to confirm the change and start the synchronization process.

Rented movies are available for viewing in the Videos app on your iPad. Tap the Rentals heading at the top of the screen and then tap your movie to begin viewing.

TV Shows, Podcasts, iTunes U, Books, and Photos

Syncing your TV shows, podcasts, iTunes U, books, and photos follows the same steps outlined in the music and movie sections. I'll discuss syncing photos between your iPad to your computer in Chapter 10.

Use iCloud to Synchronize Your Life

iCloud is an online storage and synchronization service from Apple that is tightly integrated into the iPad, iPhone, and iPod touch devices. It simplifies your life by coordinating your address book, calendars, reminders, Safari bookmarks, and photos across all your Apple devices and your computers.

Get Started with iCloud

To get the most out of iCloud, you'll want to configure its sync and storage settings on both your iPad and your computer. On your computer, iCloud requires a Mac with OS X Lion or greater or a computer with Windows Vista or Windows 7. Apple devices, like your iPad, need iOS 5 or later, which comes preinstalled on your third-generation iPad. Should you need to upgrade your computer's software, follow the manufacturer's instructions to do this.

Set Up iCloud on Your iPad

During the setup process for your iPad, you were prompted to enable iCloud for synchronization and backup. To make sure you're getting the most out of iCloud, I'm going to help you configure your synchronization and backup preferences. Tap the Settings app on your Home screen and tap the iCloud heading.

At the top of the iCloud settings window is your account settings tab. Here, you'll install your Apple ID, typically the same Apple ID you use in iTunes. Tap the Account tab to make changes or to view or change your iCloud storage plan. Your iCloud account includes 5GB of online storage for storing your contacts, calendars, portions of your iPad backups, and other documents. If you need to purchase additional storage space, you can do so here.

The remaining options in the iCloud preferences window provide options to select which types of personal information you'd like to synchronize using iCloud. I suggest enabling all the provided fields since the iCloud synchronization gives you near-instantaneous updates on all your devices. This is superior to iTunes, which would only update when you synchronize iTunes on your computer and your iPad.

iCloud synchronizes your iCloud-based e-mail, calendars, and reminders and makes them available through the iCloud web interface: www. icloud.com. Your contacts and calendars are synchronized through Address Book and iCal on the Mac and through Microsoft Outlook on Windows. Other calendar and address book contacts (Google, Yahoo!, etc.) are synchronized through that provider's synchronization system. These services are supported on the iPad, though they may require a separate setup and synchronization process.

Back Up Your iPad Using iCloud

What if, at the end of the day, you could plug in your iPad and the backup would happen automatically? That's exactly what the iCloud backup for your iPad aims to accomplish. When your iPad is plugged into a power source, locked, and connected to a Wi-Fi network, iCloud performs a nightly backup of your iPad's essential information, including accounts, document settings, and photos on your Camera Roll. However, it does not back up copies of music you've transferred from CDs or purchased from other online stores, movies, and some application data.

Here's how it works. iCloud provides unlimited free storage for music, books, TV shows, apps, and movies purchased through the iTunes Store and gives you a 5GB allowance for storing all this, plus app data (documents, in-app purchases) and device settings (Wallpaper, app organization, Mail, Contacts, and Calendar accounts). If you shoot lots of video or photos on your iPad, or have lots of documents stored on it, you may need to purchase additional iCloud storage space to ensure iCloud is able to back up all your data completely.

To enable automatic iCloud backups, tap the Storage & Backup heading at the bottom of the iCloud settings panel and slide the iCloud Backup switch to On. The advantage of iCloud backups is that your data tends to be backed up more regularly, provided you plug your iPad into a power source overnight. The downside is that it isn't quite as comprehensive as iTunes backups and could be a lot slower if you have a lot of information to back up.

In comparing your iPad backup options, iCloud provides a solid backup strategy for your most important information and relies on the use of your computer for storing any content not purchased through the iTunes Store. iTunes is more comprehensive, but requires you to plug your iPad into your computer regularly. If you're the type of person who goes months without connecting your iPad to your computer, you could be at risk of losing a lot of data if your iPad crashes, is lost, or is damaged.

If you have a smaller music and app library and want a simple, straightforward, and reliable backup service, iCloud is a great solution. iCloud is also your only backup option if you don't have a computer to use for synchronization. For users with larger music, video, and app libraries, the speed of connecting over USB instead of Wi-Fi tips the scales in favor of an iTunes backup. Know that with either option, your iPad essentials are well protected.

Set Up iCloud on Your Computer and Other Apple Devices

Now that you've enabled iCloud on your iPad, you'll want to set up iCloud on your computer and other devices to ensure they are communicating with each other and synchronizing your data.

On your computer, you'll find an iCloud control panel similar to your iPad's settings panel for controlling which data is synchronized with iCloud and your iPad.

To access the iCloud settings panel:

On Mac OS X Lion:

1. From the Apple menu at the top of the screen, select System Preferences.

2. Click the iCloud icon under the Internet & Wireless heading.

3. Sign in to iCloud using your Apple ID.

4. Select the types of content you'd like synchronized with your iPad. I suggest choosing the same options you selected on your iPad.

On Windows Vista (Service Pack 2) or Windows 7:

1. Download and install the iCloud control panel from www.apple .com/icloud/setup/pc.html.

2. From the Windows Start menu, choose Control Panel | Network And Internet | iCloud.

3. Sign in to iCloud using your Apple ID.

4. Select the types of content you'd like synchronized with your iPad. I suggest choosing the same options you selected on your iPad.

5. This step is optional, but to enable automatic downloads of items purchased through the iTunes Store, open iTunes and select Edit | Preferences | Store. In the Store Preference dialog, check the types of content you'd like automatically downloaded to your computer.

iTunes and iCloud are powerful tools to help keep the data on your iPad synchronized and safe. Although they require a little time and attention to set up initially, now that you've completed the process, you'll find they run with little to no additional attention required on your part.

4

Browse the Web with Safari

Your iPad was built to make web browsing a more engaging and interactive experience, and Safari, the app you use when surfing the Web on your iPad, delivers. In most respects, Safari behaves much like a desktop web browser. It has a URL bar for you to type a web address, a Search bar for finding information on the Web, and Forward and Back buttons that work identically to their desktop counterparts. This chapter will focus on the ways Safari on the iPad and computer differ, and I'll provide tips to make your mobile browsing experience more enjoyable and fruitful.

Get Started with Safari

To begin, tap to launch the Safari app from the dock at the bottom of your Home screen. Along the top of the screen, from left to right, you'll find Back and Forward buttons; the Bookmarks menu; the Action button used for printing or sharing webpages; your URL bar with a page refresh button; and your Search bar, a quick way to perform a web search using Google, Bing, or Yahoo! search engines (see Figure 4-1).

To begin using Safari, tap the URL bar to enter your favorite web address using the onscreen keyboard. In doing so, you'll notice two changes to the onscreen keyboard that are unique to Safari.

61

Back and   Bookmarks and   Create New
Forward   Reading List   Bookmarks Bar   Browser Tab
buttons   Action
                     button   URL bar   Search bar

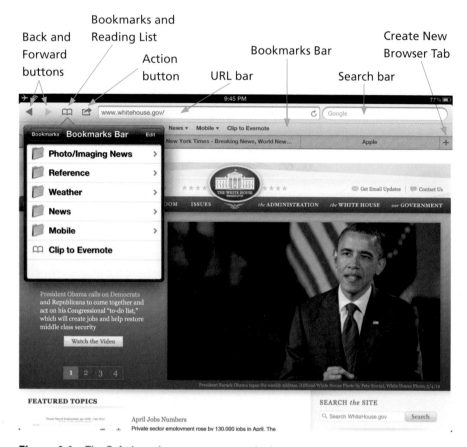

Figure 4-1   *The Safari app is your gateway to the Internet.*

First, instead of a spacebar, the bottom row of keys houses the hyphen and forward-slash keys commonly used in web addresses and a .com button to eliminate three keystrokes when typing in most URLs.

Tap and hold the .com button in the Safari onscreen keyboard to bring up a list of additional domain suffixes like .org, .edu, or .net.

Second, along the right side of the keyboard, you'll find a Go button used to confirm entry of your URL address or to trigger a web search.

When typing your URL, you can leave off the "http://www." portion of the address. Safari will insert this information automatically. For instance, typing **patagonia** will change to http://www.patagonia.com.

Remember, to browse the Web you'll need an Internet connection. Connect via Wi-Fi or cellular data network (Wi-Fi +Cellular models) as outlined in Chapter 1. The connection type your iPad is using will be listed in the top-left portion of the status bar. If you are connected to both a Wi-Fi and cellular data network, your iPad will use the Wi-Fi connection. Outside your home or office, your cellular data plan will often provide faster Internet speeds than a public Wi-Fi. If you would like to use a faster cellular network, turn off Wi-Fi in the Settings app.

Navigate the Web with Gestures

You navigate through the Web using a combination of taps, pinches, and swipes. Here are the gestures and commands you'll want to know to get the most out of Safari:

- Tap a link to follow it to another page.

- To open a link in a new tab (like a new window), tap and hold the link. Select Open In New Tab from the pop-up menu.

- Use the open-pinch gesture to enlarge a page or portion of a page. Use the closed pinch to decrease the size of the page and return to the original page view.

- Double-tap a column of text to fit the width of the text onscreen. To return to the full page view, double-tap a second time to fit the page in your web browser.

- Tap and hold the Back button to recall your recent viewing history. Slide your finger to a listing in the history to reload the page.

- To scroll within a frame on a webpage, swipe with two fingers instead of one.

- Tap and hold to preview a link's destination address. This is particularly useful if you're suspicious that the link may take you to an undesirable destination or may be a phishing attempt to trick you into revealing personal information.

Eliminate Visual Clutter with Reader

To read articles online without the distraction of flashing banner ads, slideshows, or other visual clutter, tap the Reader button on the right side of the URL bar. This brings up the Reader window and allows you to read the article as a page of clean text. For long articles, Reader will automatically load additional pages so you can enjoy an uninterrupted reading experience.

 Page 1

Is there a technological solution to global warming?

Late in the afternoon on April 2, 1991, Mt. Pinatubo, a volcano on the Philippine island of Luzon, began to rumble with a series of the powerful steam explosions that typically precede an eruption. Pinatubo had been

 Within the Reader window, you can increase or decrease the size of type on the page by using the "A" icons on the left side of the window.

Tap the Reader icon a second time to exit Reader and resume normal browsing.

Use Bookmarks to Save Time Online

Bookmarks are saved addresses of your favorite websites or sites you'd like to return to later. By bookmarking sites and organizing bookmarks into folders based on topic or use, you'll eliminate the need to remember complex web addresses, save time finding your favorite recipe, and be able to save the article that you just don't have time to read right now.

Safari uses bookmarks in the same way as your favorite browser on your computer. However, there are a few iPad-specific tips to make bookmarks more effective and minimize the amount of typing you need to perform when navigating the Web.

Synchronize Bookmarks with iCloud

Your previously saved bookmarks from a desktop version of Safari or from Safari on your iPhone should already be synchronized with your iPad using the iCloud settings we established in Chapter 3, and should appear in the Bookmarks menu to the left of the URL bar at the top of your iPad's screen.

If your bookmarks haven't transferred over, check your iCloud settings on both your iPad and your computer to ensure you've enabled bookmarks to sync over iCloud. See Chapter 3 for a review.

If you use a browser other than Safari and would like to copy your bookmarks to your iPad, use the Export option within your browser to export a copy of your bookmarks; then import those bookmarks into a desktop version of Safari. Once in Safari, your bookmarks will be synchronized over to the iPad using iCloud.

Create and Use Bookmarks in Safari

To visit a bookmarked site, tap the Bookmarks icon to open the Bookmarks listing. Here, you'll find Bookmarked Sites (indicated with the open-book icon) or Bookmarks Folder (indicated with a folder icon). Tap the Bookmarks Folder to reveal the bookmarks contained inside, or tap directly on a bookmark to open the page in Safari.

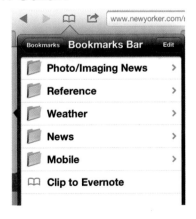

To create a bookmark of the current page, tap the Action button immediately to the left of the URL bar to call up a menu of options, as shown here.

Tap Add Bookmark to open the Add Bookmark menu. In the top field, you can type a title for the bookmark, or accept the page title as it appears in Safari and, at the bottom of the menu, specify a folder you'd like the bookmark saved to.

Safari stores and displays bookmarks in three locations allowing you to prioritize bookmarks based on their intended use:

- **Bookmarks Bar**   This slender strip of Safari real estate is reserved for your most commonly used bookmarks. Tap in the URL bar on a page to reveal the bookmarks contained in the Bookmarks Bar. You can store a folder of bookmarks within the Bookmarks Bar as well. Indicated with a small triangle to the right of the listing, tap the heading to reveal the bookmarks nested inside.

  If you'd like the Bookmarks Bar to always be visible, go to Settings | Safari and slide the Always Show Bookmarks Bar switch to On.

  I keep a collection of my most commonly visited websites, grouped into folders in the Bookmarks Bar. These are the links to maintain and update my blog, the URL of the library's online catalog, and weather and news sites I visit on a daily basis.

- **Bookmarks List**   This is the standard repository for bookmarks. I suggest building folders to categorize bookmarks by type or subject, for example, "Recipes" or "Vacation spots."

- **Reading List**   The Reading list is used for articles you don't necessarily want to store forever, but you aren't ready to read right away. To add articles to your Reading list for later browsing, tap the Action button and select Add To Reading List. View items in your Reading list by tapping the Reading List heading at the top of your Bookmarks list.

Organize Your Bookmarks

As your bookmark collection grows, you'll want to organize, reorder, and delete bookmarks. The changes you make to your bookmarks on your iPad will be synchronized to your desktop version of Safari or your iPhone/iPad touch, so be sure the changes you make here help you stay organized on *all* your devices, not just your iPad.

Tap the Bookmarks icon to display the Bookmarks list. Tap the Edit button to modify the order of bookmarks and bookmark folders or to delete bookmarks. The three horizontal bars on the right are a clue that you can drag the items on the list to a new order, and the red-and-white circle on the list indicates you can delete an item from the list by tapping the icon and then tapping the Delete button that appears on the right.

To rename a bookmark or bookmark folder, first tap the Edit button and then the bookmark's name. This brings up the Edit Bookmark menu.

Tap in the top field to edit the bookmark or folder's name, or tap in the bottom field to select a new location for your bookmark.

To create a new folder for your bookmarks, tap the Edit menu from the Bookmarks list, tap the New Folder button to create a new folder, and enter the Edit Folder menu. Enter a name for your bookmarks folder and choose an enclosing folder from the tab at the bottom of the menu.

Tap the Done button or tap anywhere outside the Bookmarks list when you're finished editing your bookmarks.

Brilliant Browsing in Safari

Now that you're beginning to get beyond the basics and understand what Safari can do, it's time to look at some of the more advanced ways you can put Safari to use in improving your web experience.

Use Tabs to View Multiple Pages

Safari uses tabs instead of multiple browser windows to display multiple webpages. This is similar to the Tabs feature found on many desktop browsers. To create a new tabbed window, tap the plus sign (+) icon just below the Search bar. After you begin using tabs, you can tap and hold the + icon to show a list of recently closed tabs, which is useful for opening a window you've accidentally closed.

Tap the tab heading to jump between tabbed windows, or tap the X on the left side of the tab to close the window.

Copy Images from Webpages

If you need to copy an image from a webpage for your daughter's book report or other noncommercial use, tap and hold the image. In the pop up menu that appears, select Save Image to save the photo to your Photo Album.

Create a Shortcut to a Webpage on Your Home Screen

If you have a webpage you visit on a regular basis, like a web-based e-mail account or your stock portfolio, you can save the page's URL as an icon on your Home screen for quicker access.

Enter the webpage into your browser that you wish to create the shortcut for. Tap the Action button to the left of the URL bar, and select Add To Home Screen. In the Add To Home Screen button, customize the title of the shortcut and then tap Add to create an icon on your Home screen.

Sharing Webpages via E-mail or Twitter

Did you find a mind-altering article you want to share with your social network, or do you want to share your travel plans with relatives? The Action button allows you to quickly share a web address using Twitter or Email.

To send a webpage via Twitter, tap the Action button, tap Tweet, and, if prompted, sign in using your Twitter account user name and password. Tweets are limited to 140 characters, so Safari compresses the web address to save more characters for writing. The number of characters you have remaining for your tweet is indicated in the lower-right corner of the Tweet window. Tap Send when you're happy with your social media missive.

To deliver the web address via Email, tap the Action button and select Mail Link To This Page. In the resulting window, enter the e-mail address(es) of your recipients and add a brief message. By default, the e-mail will be sent using your iCloud address. If you'd prefer to use another account, tap twice on the CC/BCC, From heading in the e-mail and then tap one of the alternate e-mail addresses listed in the pop-up menu. Tap Send to deliver your e-mail.

I'll go into much more depth discussing e-mail and the Mail app in Chapter 5 and Twitter and social media in Chapter 11.

Use Safari's Hidden Features

Safari has a few remaining features for you to explore that are
predominantly hidden from view. While these are less frequently used
than other features covered in this chapter, they are still handy to have
in your bag of tricks.

Quickly Scroll to the Top of the Page

To quickly scroll to the top of a long page of text, tap the status bar,
the thin black bar at the top of the screen.

Save to Contacts

Are you looking at the website of a new business connection you'd like
to add to your contacts list? Navigate to a page displaying your new
colleague's phone number, tap the number, and choose Add To
Contacts from the pop-up menu. In the Info menu, you can choose to
create a new contact from the phone number or add to an existing
contact. The one drawback with this technique is that the Contacts
menu has a tendency to obscure the rest of the address on the page,
making it difficult to enter the address and other information (and this
window can't be repositioned).

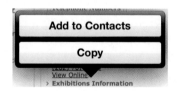

Find Specific Text on a Page

Are you quickly scanning a text-heavy page looking for a specific word,
phrase, or piece of information? Tap in the Search bar and then enter
the word or phrase you're looking for in the Find On Page field at the
top of the onscreen keyboard. Safari will automatically highlight the
text matching your search on the page. The two arrows to the right of
the Find On Text field allow you to jump to the previous/next instance
of the word on the page. Tap Done on the left side of the keyboard or
the keyboard key.

Use Dictate to Browse the Web

Don't forget that the Dictation app embedded in your keyboard is a great tool for using speech to conduct a web search. Tap in the text field appropriate to the text you'll be entering, and then tap the Dictation icon on your keyboard. Speak your selection, and then tap the Dictation icon a second time to translate your speech to text. Tap Go or Search on the onscreen keyboard to enter your selection or trigger your search.

Configure Safari's Preferences

Safari has its own preferences panel within the Settings app. Here, you'll find several options to fine-tune your Safari experience, protect yourself from malicious websites, and control the information websites store about your browsing habits.

Tap the Settings app from your Home screen, and then tap the Safari heading to open Safari's preferences.

Safari	
General	
Search Engine	Google >
AutoFill	Off >
Open New Tabs in Background	ON
Always Show Bookmarks Bar	OFF
Privacy	
Private Browsing	OFF
Accept Cookies	From visited >
Clear History	
Clear Cookies and Data	
Security	
Fraud Warning	ON
Warn when visiting fraudulent websites.	
JavaScript	ON
Block Pop-ups	ON

Fill Out Web Forms Faster with AutoFill

AutoFill uses your name, address, phone number, and e-mail address stored in your personal contact within Address Book to quickly enter this information into a web form. To activate this feature, tap AutoFill and then move the Use Contact Info slider to On. Tap My Info to bring up a list of contacts from your Address Book and navigate to your entry in the list.

If you'd like to have Safari remember the user names and passwords for sites you visit, move the Names And Passwords slider to On. If at any point you worry about the safety of storing this information on your iPad, you can tap the Clear All button to erase it from your iPad's memory.

Refine Safari's Tabs and Bookmark's Bar

The Open New Tabs In Background option allows you to specify whether you'd like new browser tabs you create to open in the foreground, meaning the new page becomes active immediately, or whether it opens in the background, with your original page continuing to appear on your screen.

The Always Show Bookmarks bar keeps the Browser Bar visible at all times, eliminating the need to tap the URL bar to display these commonly used bookmarks.

Protect Your Online Privacy

Safari's preferences also give you options to help protect your privacy and personal information when browsing.

Leave No Trace with Private Browsing

Are you shopping for a gift for your spouse or surprising your child with a great vacation? Enable the Private Browsing option to ensure the pages you visit won't appear in Safari's history tab or appear as AutoFill options when someone begins typing a web address in the URL bar.

When Private Browsing is enabled, Safari's gray user interface elements turn black to serve as a visual reminder of your stealth surfing status.

If you've forgotten to enable Private Browsing and need to erase the pages you've visited from Safari's history, tap the Clear History option to erase all websites from Safari's history. Because this resets your history, making it harder to return to sites you'd want to go back to, you'll have to confirm your selection before your history is erased.

Sweep Out Cookies

Cookies are small packets of information websites store on your computer or mobile device to preserve information you've entered into the site, user names or passwords you've entered, or items on an e-commerce site you've looked at or added to a shopping cart. In addition, websites use cookies to track the behaviors and patterns of visitors to their site.

To see which websites are storing cookies and data on your iPad, tap the Advanced heading at the bottom, and then tap Website Data to see a list of the sites storing cookie data on your iPad. To delete website data from a single site, swipe from left to right across the website's heading and then tap the Delete button.

If you'd like to delete all cookies stored on your iPad, tap the Clear Cookies And Data heading and then confirm the deletion in the resulting alert window.

Safari Security

The three remaining preferences aim to make your online experience a more secure one. Fraud Warning works to detect fraudulent websites or attempts to steal your private information. JavaScript, a popular web programming language used for adding interactivity and deep functionality to websites, can be enabled or disabled here. While there are occasions where JavaScript can be used maliciously within a webpage, disabling this feature will dramatically limit the functionality of all but the simplest webpages. For this reason, I suggest leaving it on.

Last, the Block Pop-ups tab hides annoying pop-up advertisements, though some sites have figured out how to open the pop-up in another tab, bypassing this feature.

As you can see, Safari has a wealth of features to make browsing on the iPad an efficient and enjoyable experience. With so much great content online, and a beautiful screen to view that content on, it's no wonder the iPad is such a popular tool for browsing the Web.

5

Masterful E-mail
on Your iPad

Along with surfing the Web, sending and receiving e-mail is one of
the most popular uses of the iPad. However, syncing your e-mail
with your computer and other devices can cause headaches. Never
fear—in this chapter, I'll help you configure your e-mail accounts
correctly for use on the iPad and give you a tour of the unique features
of Mail. As with the previous chapter, I'll assume you're familiar working
with desktop e-mail applications and I won't spend a lot of time on the
features common to both platforms. Instead, I'll focus on helping you
manage e-mail on multiple devices, discuss the difference between
Fetch and Push message retrieval, and show you how to remove the
"Sent from my iPad" signature from every message you send.

Add Your E-mail Accounts to Mail

During the setup process, when you entered your Apple ID, you
triggered the setup process for your iCloud e-mail account as well. If
you only use your iCloud e-mail address, *yourname*@me.com, you're
ready to begin using Mail, the iPad's e-mail app.
However, many of us have multiple e-mail addresses for
work and personal correspondence. Therefore, it pays
to add these e-mail addresses to Mail so you can have
all your Inboxes at your fingertips.

To add a new e-mail account to your iPad, go to the Settings app on your Home screen and tap the Mail, Contacts, Calendars heading in the left column. At the top of the Mail, Contacts, Calendars preferences pane, tap Add Account to open the Add Account setup menu. Tap the type of e-mail account you'd like to add. If you are not using one of the common web-based services or a Microsoft Exchange e-mail account, tap the Other tab at the bottom of the list.

The Mail setup process handles the technical configuration of your e-mail accounts automatically. You only need to provide basic information about the account.

The information you need to provide will vary slightly, depending on the type of account you're setting up. The following steps are used for Gmail, Yahoo!, and AOL—the most frequently used accounts.

1. Begin by adding your name to the Name text field. This will be the name that your e-mail recipients will see in the From heading in their e-mail application.

2. In the E-mail field, enter the existing e-mail address you'd like to add to Mail.

3. In the Password field, enter the password for the e-mail address you're adding.

4. In the Description field, give your account a name like "Work," "Gmail," or "Personal" to help you identify the account in the Mail app.

5. Tap the Next button to complete the setup. Your iPad will connect with your e-mail provider to verify your account settings and, when successful, will activate your account.

6. In the next window, specify what types of information (Mail, Contacts, Notes) you'd like synchronized with your iPad and whether you'd like messages archived to the iPad.

7. Tap Save to complete the setup of your e-mail account.

Should you have any difficulties establishing your e-mail account, visit www.apple.com/support/ipad/assistant/mail/ for specific instructions on resolving common problems.

Repeat the setup process for each e-mail account you wish to add to your iPad.

Synchronize E-mail Across Devices

Setting up your e-mail accounts using the method described earlier is usually straightforward. Getting your e-mail to sync across devices, however, can be a little more difficult and can be a source of frustration. You may find you have to delete the same message on each of your devices, or, if you read a message on one device, you're unable to retrieve it on another. Fortunately, all you need to do is change the mail delivery protocol used by your e-mail service provider from POP (Post Office Protocol) to IMAP (Internet Message Access Protocol). IMAP accounts retain e-mail messages on an e-mail server. Any changes you make to an e-mail message on one device (e.g., read the message) are honored by all other devices. POP e-mail accounts copy the message from a central server to a device and changes you make to the message status are stored on the device, not the server. For example, if you download a message from a POP account, read it on your iPad, and leave it as a read message in your Inbox, it will be missing when you access your e-mail account from your laptop because your iPad effectively "possesses" the only copy of the e-mail.

To change your e-mail's status from POP to IMAP, you'll need to go to the e-mail service itself. For web-based e-mail accounts like Gmail, changing your account type from POP to IMAP is a straightforward process, though you may have to do a little digging to find the correct settings. If your e-mail is provided by a corporate entity, or if you do not have direct access to the account, you may need to contact your IT help desk or customer support service to make the change.

 If you're unable to change your e-mail account type from POP to IMAP, you can configure your iPad to leave messages on the server so they can be accessed from other devices. Check out http://support.apple .com/kb/HT3228 for detailed instructions.

Get Acquainted with the Mail App

Now that your e-mail accounts are set up on the iPad and you've checked to be sure all your e-mail accounts are IMAP instead of POP accounts, it's time to start working with Mail, the e-mail application on the iPad.

Tap the Mail icon to launch the app. When the iPad is held horizontally, Mail uses a split-column view to provide lots of room for you to read your messages, as well as ease of navigation between e-mail accounts. The left column in the split-column view serves to help you navigate between multiple e-mail accounts and the messages in your Inbox. When held vertically, only the current message is displayed. Use the Inbox button at the top-left corner of the screen to slide open a drawer containing your messages and Inboxes.

When you first open Mail, the left column will show your Inboxes and corresponding e-mail accounts. Because you'll spend most of your time working through your Inbox, the Mail app places your Inbox(es) at the top of the column along with an All Inboxes option to view a collection of all e-mails in your Inboxes.

Tap All Inboxes to view the messages in the Inboxes of all your e-mail accounts. Tap any message in the left panel to bring up the message in the viewer on the right. E-mail threads are automatically grouped together, and the number of images in the thread is indicated with a white-and-gray square and a right-pointing arrow. Tap the message in the message viewer to reveal individual e-mails within the thread.

The buttons along the top provide the key functions you'd expect from any e-mail application. Key features are indicated in Figure 5-1 and described from left to right:

- **Mailboxes/Inbox**   This button is used for navigating up to the next organizational level within the Mail app. A standard navigational convention on the iPad, this button is used to bring you to the previous screen or level of options.

- **Move**   The Move button provides another means of transferring an e-mail to another folder.

- **Trash/Archive**   This icon will change depending upon the currently active e-mail account. Your iCloud account displays a trashcan icon, and a Gmail-based account displays an archive icon. In either case, tap the icon to remove the message from your Inbox.

- **Reply/Reply All/Forward/Print**   Tap the reply arrow and select the appropriate option from the pop-up menu.

- **New Message**   Compose a new e-mail message. Read on for tips for composing and sending e-mail.

- **Check for New Messages**   In the bottom-left corner of the Mail app is the Check For New Messages icon. Tap to check for new e-mails in all your accounts. To the right of the button is a display indicating the last time Mail checked the e-mail servers for new messages.

Reply/Reply All/Forward/Print

Trash/Archive   New

Move   Message

Mailboxes/Inbox

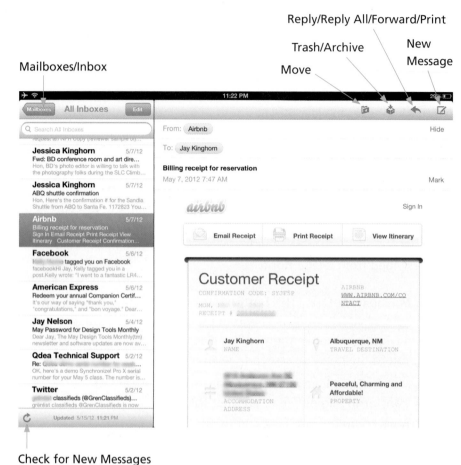

Check for New Messages

Figure 5-1   *The Mail app opened to show all inbox messages*

The Edit button reveals three important options highlighted in Figure 5-2: Delete, Move, and Mark. For the following instructions, you'll need to first tap Edit to reveal the options described.

- **Delete/Archive**   This button allows you to delete several messages at a time by tapping the blank circle to the left of the message heading. The red check box indicates these messages are marked for deletion. Tap Delete to send the messages to the trash. Certain e-mail accounts archive messages instead of deleting them. For these accounts, the Delete button will be labeled Archive, as shown in Figure 5-2.

Delete/Archive   Move   Mark

Figure 5-2 *Tap the Edit button to move, delete, or mark multiple e-mails.*

To delete or archive an individual message, swipe your finger from left to right over the e-mail header. A red Delete button appears to the right of the header. Tap it to delete the message.

- **Move**   This button allows you to move a single message or group of messages to a given folder within your e-mail account.

  As with the Delete option, tap in the blank circle to the left of the messages you plan to move, and then tap Move. The left panel automatically shifts to show the list of available folders within your account. Tap a folder to move the messages to this new location. I recommend performing a test to ensure your folders and messages sync across all your devices before you begin sorting all your e-mail messages into folders.

- **Mark**   Flag important messages or mark them as unread to return to at a later time. Tap the blank circles to select a message, then tap Mark, and from the pop-up menu choose either Flag or Mark As Unread.

Compose and Send E-mails

Now that you're acquainted with the layout of the Mail app, I'll turn my focus to the task that you use Mail for the most: composing new

e-mail messages and replying to the ones in your Inbox. First, tap the
Compose E-mail button to create a new message.

Add Recipients from Contacts

Tap in the To field to begin manually typing recipients for your e-mail.
Mail will auto-fill e-mail addresses from the contacts in your address
book as well as your Mail database. If you'd prefer to select a recipient
from a list of contacts, tap the + button on the right side of the
message to display a list of your contacts with a helpful search field at
the top. Tap the contact to select an e-mail address from their address
book card. Repeat either method or manually type addresses separated
with a comma to add multiple recipients.

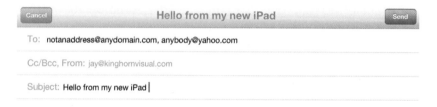

Unfortunately, there is no easy way to add a group of e-mail
recipients directly within the Mail app. However, there are a few
workarounds to consider:

- Copy and paste the e-mail addresses from a note or other text
  document into the To field of your e-mail.

- Purchase a third-party app like Group E-mail! from the App
  Store to build and manage group e-mail lists.

Mail sends new messages from your default e-mail account, although
you can change this. For now, provided you have more than one e-mail

account connected to Mail, when you want to change the account used to send a single e-mail, tap the CC/BCC/From heading to separate the fields, and then tap the From heading to display a pop-up menu of all your e-mail addresses. Tap the address you'd like to use for this message and then return to composing your e-mail.

Add a subject to the Subject line, and tap in the body of the text to look at some of the ways you can speed up the process of typing your e-mail.

Tips to Compose E-mail with Style and Ease

I've already discussed the limitations of the onscreen keyboard, so any shortcuts you can take to minimize the number of characters you need to type to communicate your message to your recipient, the better off (and faster) you'll be.

The fastest way to compose e-mails is to use the Dictation app to convert your speech to text. As a reminder, be sure to speak your punctuation, like "Dear Joe comma" to write "Dear Joe,". In multiline e-mails, saying the phrase "new line" will begin the next phrase on another line. Saying the words "new paragraph" will add a full carriage return between paragraphs, making for a clean, easy-to-read e-mail.

Whether you're dictating your e-mails or typing by hand, you'll probably still need to perform some manual text cleanup. Here are a few tips to speed up the process:

- With text created by the Dictation app, a blue underline indicates text Dictation thinks may be an inaccurate translation.

  Sometimes dictation is puzzled
  with a blue highlight

- Tap and hold to activate the onscreen magnifying glass to accurately position your cursor between letters.

- In typed text, look for a red underline to indicate misspelled words. Tap the word to highlight it and bring up suggestions for correctly spelled words.

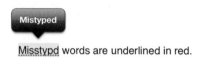

Misstypd words are underlined in red.

- As you type the first few characters of a word, the intelligent keyboard will suggest the completed word in blue below your current line of text. Tap the spacebar to accept the word.

- Hidden behind several keys on your onscreen keyboard are several quick keys. Swiping up on the comma key inserts an apostrophe. Performing the same action on the period key adds a quotation mark. Swiping up on the hyphen key adds an em-dash (a double hyphen).
- Double-tap the shift keys to activate caps lock, but please don't overdo caps in your e-mails. It looks as though you are shouting.
- Shake your iPad to undo your last action.

Format Text for Flourish and Clarity

Most of Mail's formatting tools are hidden from view, leading many iPad users to believe they don't exist. In fact, the iPad has a comprehensive set of tools to format your text for clarity, emphasis, and to include foreign or special characters.

Add Bold, Italic, or Underline Formatting   Tap a word to select it, and then extend the selection bars to include all the text you'd like to format. In the pop-up edit menu, tap the right-pointing triangle to access additional formatting features. Tap the **B/U** icon to display the formatting options. Tap your preferred choice to format your text.

Em-dashes, En-dashes, Hyphens, and Ellipses   Tap and hold the hyphen key to bring up a menu with an em-dash, en-dash, and bullet. Slide your finger to the desired symbol to insert it. To add ellipses, tap and hold the period key. Slide your finger to the ellipses to insert it into your text.

Accented and Special Characters   Tap and hold any of the following keys to pull up a list of alternate characters, like accented letters, monetary symbols, or special characters: A, C, E, I, L, N, O, S, U, Y, Z, 0 (zero), $, &, ?, !, ', ", and %. Slide your finger to the alternate character to insert it into your text.

Send E-mails with Attachments

Another weakness of the iPad's Mail app is its ability, or lack thereof, to easily send e-mails with attachments. To send an e-mail with an attachment, say, a photo or a PDF document, you need to send it from the app used to edit or store the photo or document. The third-party app Group E-mail! provides an interface with access to a variety of file sources on your iPad and makes it easy to attach multiple files to a single recipient or e-mail group.

Manage Your Inbox

For many busy professionals, e-mail is the primary means of communicating with coworkers, clients, and even friends you don't see face to face regularly. As a result, many people seem to *live* in their Inbox. This makes it particularly important to navigate through the incoming mountain of e-mail quickly and effectively.

Read and Delete Messages at a Glance

One of the keys to dealing with an ever-growing Inbox is to be able to quickly scan thorough your messages to see which ones can be deleted immediately. To make this easier, you'll want to change Mail's preference to preview more of the message within your Inbox's column view.

1. Tap your Home button to exit Mail and return to the Home screen.

2. Navigate to your Settings app and tap Mail, Contacts, Calendars.

3. Below the Mail heading, tap Preview and select the number of lines within the e-mail you'd like to preview in your Inbox.

If you work in an office where you're copied on lots of e-mails that you have to read but not respond to, increasing the length of the preview may allow you to read the full contents of the e-mail without actually opening it in the main window. Within this column view, you can quickly delete any message that doesn't require a response. To do this:

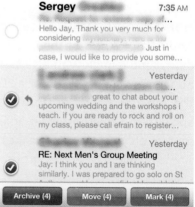

1. Tap the Edit button in the top-right corner of your Inbox.

2. Click the empty circle to the left of any message you'd like to delete.

3. Tap the Delete button to erase or archive the selected messages.

Read Messages, Preview Attachments, and Take Action

One hallmark of several popular productivity methodologies is to take action on any item, including e-mail, that requires less than two minutes to respond. Keep this in mind as you begin making your way through the remaining e-mails in your Inbox.

To deliver a quick reply or forward the e-mail to another recipient, tap the Reply button in the menu bar at the top and select the appropriate item from the pop-up menu.

Create Shortcuts for Common Responses

In Chapter 2 I introduced you to shortcuts: simple strings of text you type that are automatically replaced with a longer phrase or sentence, like your name, a common e-mail signature, or a lengthy (and easily mistyped) technical term. You can also use shortcuts to quickly insert boilerplate text into an e-mail. This allows you to respond to support queries or point to additional online information without a lot of extra typing.

To create a shortcut:

1. Tap the Home button to exit Mail and return to the Home screen.

2. Navigate to the Settings app, tap it, and then tap the General heading and then Keyboard.

3. Under the Shortcuts heading, tap Add New Shortcut and in the resulting window, type the phrase you'd like to appear in your e-mail along with the shortcut used to trigger the text replacement.

4. Tap Save in the upper-right corner to save your shortcut.

 When creating shortcuts, think of shortcut keys you can type quickly. Although it's tempting to create shortcuts around capital letters, like "SPT" for support, it is faster to type the lowercase "spt" and eliminates possible errors.

Review and Save Attachments

The Mail app can preview attachments in the most commonly used file formats directly within the Mail window. You can download and preview attachments simply by tapping them. Many common image formats can be previewed directly within the body of the e-mail. Depending upon the size of the attachment, you may need to tap the attachment icon to prompt Mail to download the attached file from the server. Smaller files are downloaded immediately on a Wi-Fi connection, while larger items must be downloaded manually.

AQ March 2009.doc
201 KB

To save your attachment from the preview window, tap the Action icon in the upper-right corner and select Open In <Application Name> to open the attachment in the file's creating application (or closest equivalent), or select Open In to choose from a list of apps that support the attachment's file format.

For file types that are not supported natively on the iPad (Microsoft Office documents, for example), tap and hold the attachment icon. From the pop-up menu, choose to open it in a specific application, or use the Quick Look option to preview the document from within Mail.

To save image attachments, tap the Reply button within the main body of the Mail app and select Save Image to save the attached image in your photo library. If you'd prefer to save a single image, tap and hold the image icon and choose Save Image from the pop-up menu.

Pull Information from an E-mail

Working efficiently in Mail on the iPad requires you to think creatively of ways you can minimize typing. Fortunately, Mail has a few additional tricks up its sleeve to help you harvest information from the body of an e-mail to create contacts or appointments on your calendar or to locate an address on a map, all things that minimize the need to type.

Create Contacts from Addresses and Phone Numbers

If an e-mail message contains contact information, like a phone number or address, you'd like to use to create a new contact or add to an existing contact in your address book, tap the phone number or tap and hold the address. From the pop-up menu, choose Add To Contacts. The copied information will be presented along with the options Create New Contact or Add To Existing Contact. If you choose Add To Existing Contact, another pop-up menu will appear to display a list of your current contacts.

Find Locations on a Map

When you tap an address within an e-mail, the address will be displayed within the Maps app. You can also tap and hold the address to choose between adding the address to your Contacts database and displaying the location on a map.

In the Map view, tap the red pin denoting your destination to display a menu that allows you to search for directions to or from your destination, add the location to your Contacts database, share the location via e-mail or Twitter, or add the location to your Maps bookmarks of favorite places.

Add Dates to Your Calendar

If an e-mail contains the dates and times an event will occur, you'll find this information highlighted in blue text with an underline, indicating a hyperlink. Tap the highlighted text and select Show In Calendar if you'd like to see whether or not you're free for the appointment, or tap Create Event to create a Calendar event, invite others to the meeting, and trigger an alert to remind you prior to the meeting.

Don't forget, you have a massage appointment next tuesday at 5 pm.

 Your information in an e-mail doesn't have to be written out in a literal time/date format for the Mail app to understand your intent and create a calendar event. For instance, if your friend sends you an e-mail with the text, "Let's meet for coffee next Wednesday," Mail will create a calendar event for the following Wednesday.

As you can see, digging a little below the surface of the Mail app reveals a surprising amount of intelligence to help you get through your Inbox and link the information within your e-mails to other commonly used apps.

Six Tips for a Better E-mail Experience

In this section, I'll help you modify Mail's preferences for better productivity, add your preferred e-mail address to Notification Center, and give you a quick tip to help you stem the tide of e-mails while on vacation.

See Important E-mails in Your Notification Center

The Notification Center automatically displays e-mails from your iCloud e-mail address and allows you to quickly scan your Inbox from any app or screen on the iPad. For most users, this isn't their most frequently used e-mail address. To make messages from all your e-mail addresses appear in Notification Center:

1. Visit https://appleid.apple.com/ and click Manage Your Account.

2. Log in using your Apple ID.

3. In the Alternate E-mail Addresses section, enter your e-mail addresses. Be sure to use the + icon at the bottom of the screen to create new e-mail form fields.

4. Apple will send you an e-mail to confirm each of your accounts. Follow the directions in the e-mail(s) to verify your new e-mail address.

This change should take place within a few minutes and your messages will display in Notification Center.

Choose Between Push and Fetch Message Retrieval

Push and Fetch are e-mail message retrieval options you specify within the Mail, Contacts, Calendars portion of the Settings app. Because these are not commonly used terms, I want to provide you with a quick overview before we go in to Settings to make any changes.

On a basic level, Push sends notifications to your iPad that there are new messages on the server, causing Mail to connect with the server, grab the e-mails, and make them available to you. Push delivery gives you a more immediate e-mail response and is ideal for those who want to be notified of a new e-mail as soon as it arrives in their Inbox. Not all e-mail accounts support Push. For example, my Gmail-based accounts only give me the option of selecting Fetch delivery. Microsoft Exchange accounts and your iCloud account do support Push and make it available to you as an option within your settings.

The downside of using Push is that it can deplete your batteries more quickly than the alternative, Fetch. Fetch checks with the e-mail server at specified intervals, every 15 minutes, for example, to see if there are new messages. If there are new messages, they are downloaded and made available inside Mail. Setting Fetch to a longer interval, say every hour, will help your battery last longer. Of course, you'll have to balance battery life with your e-mail management habits to find a combination that works well for you.

To adjust your e-mail message retrieval options:

1. Tap the Settings app, and then tap the Mail, Contacts, Calendars heading.

2. Tap the Fetch New Data heading.

3. Use the slider to turn Push on or off, or tap your desired interval for fetching e-mail from the servers (15 Min, 30 Min, Hourly, or Manual).

In the Advanced heading at the bottom of the Fetch New Data preferences, you're able to specify Fetch or Push notification individually for each of your e-mail accounts.

Change Your Default Account

While you're in the Settings app looking at your Mail, Contacts, Calendars settings, it is worth taking a moment to change your default e-mail account from your iCloud/Apple address, *yourname@me.com*, to another, more frequently used account. The default address is used when working with your Inbox that includes messages from multiple accounts. It is also used when you send an e-mail from outside of Mail, when e-mailing a webpage, for example.

Change your default e-mail address with a quick tap on the Default Account heading within the Mail, Contacts, Calendars preferences panel. In the resulting window, tap the account you'd like to set as your default address.

Stop Using the "Sent from My iPad" Signature

I prefer my e-mails to be free of "Sent from my iPad" or "Sent from my iPhone" signatures. So one of the first things I did with my new third-generation iPad was remove this default signature.

To do this, access the Settings app, tap the Mail, Contacts, Calendars heading, and then tap the Signature heading. In the resulting dialog, type the e-mail signature you'd like to use for all of your outgoing messages. This could be a mind-expanding quote, a list of your contact information, or just leave it blank.

Temporarily Stop Delivery of E-mail to Your Account

Are you a habitual e-mail checker who can't stop looking at your Inbox even when you're on vacation? Yeah, me too. If you'd like to help yourself enjoy your vacation more thoroughly, temporarily disable the delivery of e-mails to your accounts.

To do this, be sure you're still in the Mail, Contacts, Calendars portion of your Settings app, and then tap an e-mail account at the top of the window. Swipe the Mail slider from On to Off to stop receiving e-mails. When you return from your enjoyable and uninterrupted vacation, swipe it back to the On position to resume normal delivery.

Configure Mail's Sounds

Would you prefer not to hear the swoosh sound when you send an e-mail? Or would you like to be notified with an air raid siren when a new message lands in your Inbox? Jump over to the General settings heading within the Settings app and tap Sounds. Here, you'll see headings for New Mail and Sent Mail. Tap each one to display a list of available sounds/ringtones and an option to purchase additional ringtones from the iTunes Store using the Buy More Tones button at the top of the screen. For only $0.99 you can have Chewbacca herald the arrival of new messages or have Adele enchant outgoing e-mails. Who knew that sorting through your Inbox could be this entertaining?

Well, there you have it. Your e-mail accounts are set up, ready to use, and customized to suit your specific needs. I know e-mail is one of the most important, and commonly used, features on the iPad. As you work more with your iPad, you may want to return to this chapter to take advantage of some of the time-saving tips contained at the end of the chapter. By then, you'll have a better idea of how you're using e-mail on your iPad and what modifications you can make to Mail so it's an even stronger tool for you.

6

Organize Your Life with Calendar, Contacts, and Reminders

Let me introduce you to an immensely useful trio of Apple apps that will help you stay in control of your busy life: Calendar, Contacts, and Reminders. When used together, these apps work seamlessly to help you plan meetings, arrive on time, and stay in touch. You'll find these organizational apps to be well matched to the iPad's strengths and possibly even hard to live without.

Plan Your Life with Calendar

Calendar is the iPad's calendaring and scheduling app used to keep you organized and on time. If you'd like to stay in sync with your iPad and computer, Calendar uses iCloud or iTunes to synchronize with Microsoft Outlook on Windows and iCal on the Mac. Calendar also allows you to synchronize your web-based Microsoft Exchange, Google, and Yahoo! calendar accounts. In doing so, Calendar provides you with all of the important details of your day and allows you to keep on top of your time commitments.

Calendar at a Glance

Calendar provides five different views for looking at your appointments. From the hour-by-hour perspective of the Day view to the bird's-eye view of the Year view, you can view and sort your schedule a number of different ways. As shown in Figure 6-1, consistent toolbars on the top and bottom of the screen allow you to view specific calendars, accept or decline invitations delivered to you via e-mail, search for details of an appointment, or add a new appointment to your calendar.

Figure 6-1   *The Calendar app provides several different ways to view the events on your calendar.*

To start, tap the Calendar app that's already loaded on your iPad. Tap the Month button, just below the clock in the status bar, and then tap the Today button in the lower-left corner of the screen. The Today button provides a convenient way to quickly bring your calendar back to the present day, regardless of which calendar view you're in. To navigate between pages on the calendar, whether they are days, weeks, months, or years, swipe from right to left to move forward, or reverse the gesture to move backward in time. Or, navigate using the time bar at the bottom.

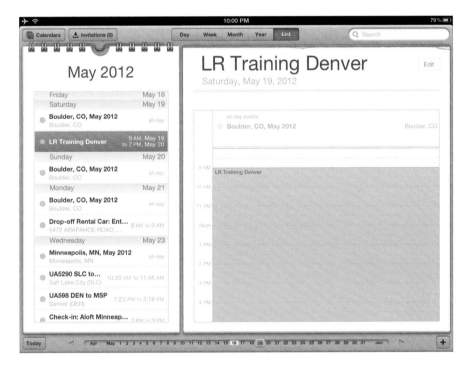

The List view shows only your appointments, listed in chronological order. Swiping left or right in this view jumps between appointments, not days. So, if you have four appointments on Tuesday and nothing until Friday, you'll need to swipe four times to get through Tuesday's events, and the fifth will take you directly to Friday. In this way, the List view serves as an efficient task manager that I find particularly useful when planning for the week ahead.

When swiping through in List view, I recommend swiping in one of the blank spaces on the screen (right below the date, for instance) for easier swiping. I have found if you swipe in the area with the lines, you may end up scrolling through your screen instead of flipping to your next appointment. Day and Week views work similarly.

Sync Your Calendars

The Calendar app synchronizes calendars using either iTunes or iCloud. As I recommended in Chapter 3, I encourage you to use iCloud for synchronizing your calendars for more immediate updates. When using iCloud, Calendar supports desktop synchronization with iCloud, Microsoft Exchange, Google, and Yahoo! calendars as well as CalDAV, an Internet standard for web-based calendars.

   To make sure all your calendars are visible within the Calendar app, navigate through the Settings app to the Mail, Contacts, Calendars preference, and then look at the text immediately below the Accounts listing. Make sure that Calendars is listed below the appropriate account heading.

Unless otherwise noted, all Calendar settings are found within the Settings app under the Mail, Contacts, Calendars heading.

If not, tap the listing for your account and, within the next menu, slide the Calendars switch from Off to On. This will enable calendar synchronization with your iPad. Your iCloud account will perform synchronization with Microsoft Outlook (Windows) and iCal desktop calendars almost immediately. Web-based calendars like Yahoo! or Google will synchronize immediately through that provider's web services.

Manage Multiple Calendars

Your calendar can display events from multiple calendar sources, say, for example, work and personal calendars. You can assign each calendar a unique color to help you review your life's commitments quickly. To see a list of which calendars are synchronized with the Calendar app, tap the Calendars button in the top-left corner of the screen. Here,

you'll see your calendars organized by the e-mail account used for synchronization. For example, you'll have an iCloud calendar used to sync between your iPad and your computer using the iCloud online service, and you may have Gmail or Yahoo! calendar or a work calendar synchronized through a Microsoft Exchange account. All your active services are listed here. These were created when you established your e-mail accounts on your iPad.

If you'd like to disable calendar synchronization for an account, jump over to the Settings app, tap the Mail, Contacts, Calendars heading, and then, at the top of the screen, tap the account you wish to disable. In the resulting window, swipe to move the Calendars lock from On to Off and remove any events associated with that account from your calendar.

Now You Know **Add Multiple Calendars to Non-iCloud Calendars**

Most of the web-based e-mail/calendar combinations only show one calendar by default. You can enable the synchronization of multiple calendars. However, you have to do it from your account provider (e.g., Gmail, Yahoo!), not from within the iPad. It is beyond the scope of this book to show you how to set up each of the supported account types, but a web search for "<Account provider> multiple calendars iPad" should direct you to the information you need.

Within each of your account headings you may have multiple calendars associated with that account. For example, within my iCloud account, I have work and personal calendars along with an additional calendar to remind me when recurring bills are due and a fourth to store unconfirmed events. Each is color-coded so I can look at the month and easily schedule around my existing commitments. Within this pop-up menu, you can tap any of the calendar headings to remove the calendar's events from view. To restore a calendar's events, tap the heading a second time to reactivate the calendar, indicated by a check mark, or tap the Show All Calendars button at the top of the pop-up menu.

To manually update all your calendars, tap the Refresh button in the top-left corner of the Calendar pop-up window.

Add a New iCloud Calendar

To create a new iCloud-based calendar, tap the Edit button in the upper-right corner of the pop-up menu, and then tap the Add Calendar button below the iCloud heading. In the next menu, enter a name for your calendar and tap the color you'd like associated with it.

Color-Code or Rename Your Calendars

To change the name or color of an existing calendar, tap the Edit button within the pop-up menu as described earlier. Next, tap the iCloud calendar you wish to change, and then, in the Edit Calendar window, tap the name to open the onscreen keyboard and enter a new name, or tap a new color label to assign it to your calendar.

 The changes you make to your calendars here will be synchronized across to your desktop calendar application. Changes to non-iCloud accounts (e.g., Gmail, Yahoo!) are not supported from within the Calendar app. You'll need to make any changes through the calendar provider's website or software.

Add New Events to Your Calendar

As your schedule changes, add new events to your calendars with a tap on the Add Event button in the lower-right corner of the screen. In all views except Year, you can also tap and hold a location on the calendar to add an event to that time and date.

This brings up the Add Event menu, where you enter your event information including the start and end time of the event, whether the event repeats and the calendar you'd like the event added to. In addition, if your calendar allows it, you can invite others to join the event and add an alert to serve as a reminder to you before the event begins. Tap Done to confirm the event details and add it to your calendar.

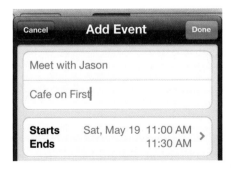

Don't forget, your calendar events for today and tomorrow appear in your Notification Center. This is a great way to see your upcoming events without the need to leave another app.

Move, Reschedule, or Delete an Event

To change the time or duration of an event without changing other details, tap and hold briefly on an event until the event listing is surrounded by a light drop shadow. This indicates the event is ready to be moved. Drag the event to a new location. In the Month view, dragging your event to a new date preserves the scheduled time. To change the scheduled time or duration, you'll need to switch to Day, Week, or List view, or tap the event and tap the Edit button from the pop-up menu. This will allow you to change any of the attributes associated with the event. If you're working in Day or Week view, you can change the date, duration, and time of an event when you tap and hold the event. Two small circles appear at the top and bottom of the event, which allow you to expand or contract the duration. You can also drag the event to another time or day. In the Day view, drag the event toward the left or right side of the screen to select a different date. In the List view, you're able to change the duration and time of the scheduled event, but not the date.

To edit all the attributes of an event in any view except Year, tap the event listing, and then tap the Edit button from the pop-up window. Update the event's information, and then tap Done to apply your changes.

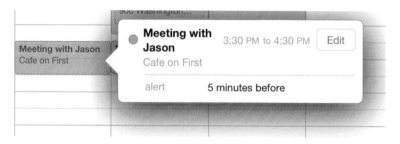

To delete an event, tap the event, tap Edit again to bring up the event's Edit menu, and then tap Delete Event from the bottom of the menu. Confirm the deletion of the event by tapping Delete Event a second time and your event is removed from your calendar.

Subscribed and Shared Calendars

Your iPad will show events for calendars you've subscribed to and allows you to display and create new events for shared calendars. It does not allow you to administer a shared calendar, subscribe to a new calendar, or create a shared calendar from within the Calendar app.

Schedule Across Time Zones

Innovation has led the human race to be highly mobile, so much so, that we find it quite easy to account for the changes in time zones when we plan to travel. When planning a meeting in a different time zone, on the East Coast, for example, I know that the 2:00 P.M. meeting we've set is on Eastern Standard Time (EST), not Mountain Standard Time (MST). However, the Time Zone support built in to the iPad is a bit too literal and, I find, counterintuitive. So, it's important to understand how the Time Zone support works in order to use this tool to your advantage, and not frustration.

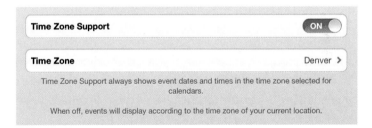

Time Zone support appears in two places on the iPad. First, you have an option to enable or disable it within the Mail, Contacts, Calendars preferences. When Time Zone support is set to Off, and your Date and Time preference is set to update based on your current location (Settings | General | Date & Time), your calendar events are always shown based on your current time zone. This can be confusing because all events shift around on your calendar as you move between time zones. For example, let's say you live in California and are flying to New York City. When you book your ticket in California, you enter the departure time of your return trip, which leaves New York at 11:00 A.M. local time. When you arrive in New York, your calendar event for your departure adjusts with the time zone, shifting from 11:00 A.M. to 2:00 P.M. A busy person may not have noticed the difference in time and would subsequently show up three hours late for their flight.

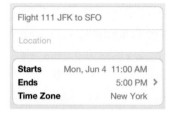

If Time Zone support is enabled for your calendars, you'll have the option to set a time zone where each event occurs. Given the preceding scenario, I specify an 11:00 A.M. departure from New York and choose New York as the time zone, and the event shows up on my calendar as departing at 8:00 A.M. while I'm still in California, then slides to the correct position when I arrive in New York.

As you can see, it's a good idea to enable Time Zone support and specify which time zone the event will take place in. This way, as you move between time zones, your calendar items will always shift based on your changing location.

As a failsafe measure, I always enter important time information, like flight departures, in the heading of the calendar event to ensure I always have a clear point of reference, regardless of where I'm located.

Calendar Productivity Tips

Of course, there are always a few tips to help you quickly move beyond the basics and make Calendar more productive for you. Here are a few I think you'll find useful.

Enter Location Information for Events

If you've never been to the location of next Tuesday's meeting, enter the address in the location field of the event. Should you need directions or get lost on the way, open your calendar, tap the event, and your event's address will be displayed next to the Edit menu. Tap the address to open the address in Maps where you can get directions to your destination. Of course, for Maps to work you do need an Internet connection via Wi-Fi or cellular network. If your calendar syncs with your smart phone, this information will be available on your phone's calendar allowing you to complete your trip without delay.

Search the Contents of Calendars

Did you store a phone number within an event that you need to retrieve to make a call? The Search bar in the upper-right corner allows you search all the information associated with any event. Tap in the Search bar and begin typing the information you wish to look for. As you type, Calendar will display a list of results matching your search criteria.

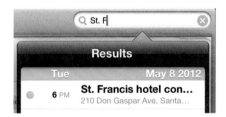

Create Recurring Events

Do you have lunch with a colleague every two weeks, or pay a bill monthly? You can set up recurring events to automatically populate your calendar so you never forget to enter an appointment.

To set up recurring events, create a new event to serve as your template for future events. In the Repeat heading of the Add Event menu, select the frequency with which the event will occur. If you make a change to a recurring event, you'll be asked whether you'd like the change to occur to only this event or all future events. Similarly, if you delete a recurring event, you'll be prompted to decide whether you'd like to delete only this event or all future events.

Invite Others to the Party (or Business Meeting)

Calendar allows you to invite others to your events as well as accept events created by others, just as you would from your desktop, with a few limitations. You can create and accept invitations using Microsoft Exchange and iCloud-based calendars, provided New Invitation Alerts is enabled within your Mail, Contacts, Calendars preferences. These services work almost identically to the desktop versions of these calendars.

Google- and Yahoo!-based calendars can accept calendar invites but cannot initiate them. I've also found problems accepting invitations from Google and Yahoo! accounts to my iCloud account. If you're working with these services, I recommend you use your web-based calendar to accept or initiate invitations. Once the event is created and the invitations sent, the event should display normally on your iPad's calendar.

An Alert for Every Event

When you create a new event, you're able to manually add an alert to remind you the event is about to take place. If you add alerts to a majority of the events on your calendar, you can specify a default alert for all of your new calendar items.

Access the Mail, Contacts, Calendars preferences, and then tap the Default Alert Times heading under the Calendars section. Here, you can specify default alerts for birthdays, events, and all-day events by tapping the heading and choosing your preferred alert time. These defaults are applied whenever you create a new event or, in the case of birthdays, whenever a birthday is detected from within your address book of contacts.

Birthdays	1 day before (9 AM) >
Events	5 minutes before >
All-Day Events	1 day before (9 AM) >

Specify Your Default Calendar

If you work with multiple calendars, you'll want to ensure that the default calendar used when you create new events is the calendar you use most often. This eliminates the step of having to manually choose your preferred calendar when you create a new appointment.

To specify your default calendar, go to the Mail, Contacts, Calendars preferences and tap Default Calendar. Tap again to set the default calendar used to create new events.

This concludes your introduction to Calendar, but before we depart, it is worth noting that many third-party apps interface with Calendar and extend the productivity power of this valuable app.

Store and Manage Your Addresses with Contacts

Contacts, your iPad's address book and contact manager, is deeply integrated into the function of several apps on the iPad. By synchronizing your iPad with your desktop addresses, entering e-mail addresses in the Mail app becomes easier; Maps and Google Earth provide directions to your friends' homes; and it becomes much easier to share photos, video, and artwork you've created with the people you care about. So, while a simple address book may not be all that cool by itself, when you think of it as a hub to connecting with your friends and colleagues online and in person, its importance takes on a whole new light.

The Contacts App at a Glance

The Contacts app is designed to mimic the look and feel of a physical address book. As shown in Figure 6-2, tabs along the left side of the screen provide quick access to a list of contacts organized alphabetically by last name or company name, while the right side displays details for a single address. Near the fold in the center of the address book, you'll find a + button for adding new contacts and an Edit button to modify the information for a given contact.

Since you've already populated your iPad with your contacts, you should have a list of contacts on the left side of the Contacts screen. If you have not yet synced your contacts with the iPad, visit Chapter 3. Tap a contact's name in the list on the left to select it. That contact's name should become highlighted in blue and the contact's information will appear on the right side of the address book. Below this contact

Figure 6-2 *The address book in Contacts should appear similar to a physical address book.*

information you'll find buttons to perform additional actions. The number of buttons displayed will depend upon the type of information you've entered for your contact and whether or not you're signed into the Messages app. We'll talk about Messages in Chapter 11.

- **Messages** Send a text or photo-based instant message over Wi-Fi or a cellular network to other iOS devices.
- **FaceTime** Provides single-button access to a video call with your contact using FaceTime.
- **Share Contact** Allows you to e-mail the contact in the commonly used vCard format.
- **Favorites** Adds your contact to your Favorites list within FaceTime. To rescind Favorite status for a contact, you'll have to go to FaceTime's Favorites list within your FaceTime app, tap the Edit button, tap the contact listing, and tap Delete.

Synchronize Your Contacts with Your Computer

The quickest way to populate your iPad's address book with all your friends, family members, and colleagues is to synchronize contacts from your computer using Address Book on Mac or Microsoft Outlook on Windows. You can sync these applications with Contacts on your iPad using either iTunes or iCloud. I prefer using iCloud for both Contacts and Calendar because it is more immediate and stores a copy of these files in the cloud that can be accessed using the iCloud website www .icloud.com. This serves as a backup copy of this information in case my iPad and computer are lost or stolen, and provides convenient access via the Web if I need to access a phone number and don't have my iPad or computer nearby.

Preview Group Contact Lists

As your contact collection grows, it makes sense to begin placing contacts in groups based on your relationship to them. This makes it much easier to find the contact you're looking for quickly. Contacts will automatically import your existing groups and sync contacts added to groups from your desktop or web-based accounts. Contacts cannot create its own groups, nor can you add contacts to or remove contacts from an existing group.

To access your groups, tap the red ribbon in the top-left corner of the address book with the Groups label. This turns the page to reveal your groups. Tap a group to return to the main address book window. The group name is indicated at the top of the left side of the page.

    All iCloud

To exit Groups without making a selection, tap the red ribbon to return to the main window.

Create a New Contact Card

Of course, syncing isn't the only way to bring your contacts into your address book. To create a new card and enter your contact's information,

Now You Know **Sync Your Google and Yahoo! Contacts to your iPad**

You can also sync contacts from Google and Yahoo! accounts through iTunes or via the Web. However, web-based synchronization for these services requires additional setup steps. For Google accounts, you'll need to set up your account using Microsoft Exchange in the Mail, Contacts, Calendars setting. For Yahoo! accounts, you need to enable CardDAV on your Yahoo! accounts and then delete and reactivate your account on the iPad. Here are links to detailed instructions for enabling synchronization on both account types:

- **Google** http://support.google.com/mobile/bin/answer .py?hl=en&answer=138740

- **Yahoo** http://help.yahoo.com/kb/index?page=content&id=SL N4922&actp=search&viewlocale=en_US&searchid=1331396759 728&locale=en_US&y=PROD_MAIL_ML

When activated, contacts from these services are listed as separate groups on the Groups page of Contacts (discussed next).

tap the + button. A new contact card will appear. Use the onscreen keyboard to enter your contact's information. For headings like Phone or Email, tap the blue heading—for example, Mobile or Home—to select an alternate label like Work. When you enter a phone number or e-mail address, a second field will appear for you to enter an alternate phone or e-mail address. If you don't need it, leave it blank. Contacts will only display fields containing information. For a few fields, like Address, a green + appears to the left of the heading, allowing you to enter a second address.

The Notes and Additional fields are particularly useful for storing information relevant to the contact. You might add a note to include the name of the person who referred you to the new contact, a client's FedEx number, or their favorite restaurant. Notes are a great way to store personalized information. However, be aware that sharing your contact via e-mail may also share the contact's associated notes.

The Add Field heading allows you to add important contact or relationship information like their spouse's or child's names, a phonetic description of their name, their Twitter or instant messaging addresses, or their birthday.

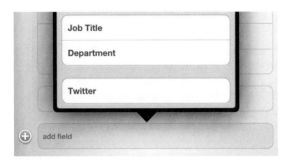

To personalize your new contact card with a photo, tap the Add Photo heading next to your contact's first and last name. In the pop-up menu, select whether you'd like to take a new photo using the back camera or select an existing photo from your photo library.

When a photo is added, tap it to scale and reposition the photo or select a different image.

To finalize creation of your new contact card, tap the Done button in the upper-right corner of the card.

Edit an Existing Card

To edit information from an existing contact card, select the card, and then tap the Edit button near the bottom of the screen, just to the right of the fold in the center of the address book. Enter new information or delete outdated info with the onscreen keyboard. Add photos, notes, or additional form fields as described earlier.

To delete a card from your address book, tap the Delete Contact button near the bottom of the card. Confirm deletion by tapping Delete in response to the alert that appears in the center of the screen.

Also at the bottom of the card in edit mode, you'll find the Link Contact button. This is used to link contacts that have been duplicated by syncing multiple accounts (e.g., iCloud and Google address books) or duplicated through the iCloud sync setup.

Tap the Done button at the top of the card to save your changes and return to your address book.

A hidden method of deleting information from a selected card is to swipe horizontally across a field within the contact. For example, sweeping your finger from left to right across a home phone number reveals a Delete button. Tap it to remove the phone number from the card, or swipe again to make the Delete button disappear.

Search and Find Contacts

Tap in the Search bar at the top of the left-facing page of Contacts to search for a specific contact in your address book. As you type, Contacts will filter your list to show possible choices that match your search. Unfortunately, Contacts is unable to search all of the fields in your address book. It searches the first and last names along with company

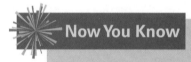

Now You Know **Remove Duplicate Cards Using Address Book on Your Desktop**

If you have created duplicate cards through the iCloud sync process and work on a Mac computer with OS X Lion 10.7, you can quickly remove duplicate contacts using the Address Book application on your desktop.

On your computer, launch Address Book and, from the Card menu, select Look For Duplicates. Address Book scans your contacts list and merges duplicate contact cards to streamline the list. This information is synchronized through iCloud, and duplicates will automatically be removed from your Contacts app on your iPad. This not only removes duplicate contacts from your address book, but also removes duplicate birthday notifications on your Calendar since these are generated by your contacts database.

names, but ignores all other fields. This is a departure from the desktop versions of the software and can limit your ability to find the contacts you're looking for, so be forewarned.

Put Contacts to Work for You

Don't let the Contacts app's appearance fool you. Although it looks like a physical address book, Contacts can do things a physical address book never could, like trigger the creation of an e-mail, launch a video call with FaceTime, or recall a webpage. Here are several tips you can use to put Contacts to work for you.

Place a Video Call with FaceTime

FaceTime is an app that allows you to make video calls when connected to a Wi-Fi network. FaceTime uses the front-facing cameras on supported iOS devices (iPhone 4 and 4S, iPad 2 and third-generation) and Mac computers running OS X Lion 10.7 to place and receive video calls.

To initiate a FaceTime video call:

1. Select a contact card from your contacts list.

2. Either tap their phone number (best for iPhones) or swipe to the bottom of the contact, tap the FaceTime button, and select an e-mail address (best for iPads or computers).

A notification will be sent to your recipient asking them if they would like to talk on FaceTime with you.

To receive a FaceTime video call, when you receive a FaceTime notification, tap the green Accept button to start the call.

 FaceTime calls to Windows computers are not supported at this time.

Create and Address an E-mail

From your contacts list you can quickly send an e-mail to one of your contacts. Select your contact from the list, and tap the e-mail address you'd like to send your message to. A New Message window will appear within Mail, preaddressed to your intended recipient. Dash off a quick note and tap Send to deliver your e-mail.

Display a Map and Get Directions

In Contacts, tap a contact's address to open the location in Maps. If you need directions, tap the Directions button in the top-left corner. By default, directions will be calculated from your current location; however, you can enter a new location by manually typing in an address or entering the name of a contact in your address book. The directions will be recalculated between the two points.

Share Your Contacts with Others

Do you need to deliver contact information for a colleague via e-mail or text message? At the bottom of the contact's details, below the Notes field, tap the Share Contact button. The contact will automatically be attached in the .vcf (Vcard) format, a widely supported standard for electronic business cards, to a new e-mail or text message.

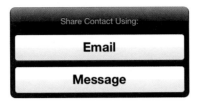

 The text message option is only available once you've entered your Apple ID in the Messages app.

Edit Your Contact Card

Before leaving the Contacts app, it is important to take a moment and verify that your contact card is up to date. Your contact card is used by many apps to personalize outgoing messages or to customize your Home screen.

First, locate your contact information within the Contacts app and make any changes to your card. Many people change the year of their birthday to mask their true age from others they share their contact with. I encourage you to add a professionally produced photograph of yourself, particularly if you plan to share your contact with other professionals at networking events or on social sharing sites.

Once you're satisfied with your card, exit Contacts and jump over to the Mail, Contacts, Calendars preferences. Under the Contacts heading, tap My Info, and verify your name and contact card are listed in this heading. If not, tap the heading and select your contact card from the pop-up menu.

Adjust Contacts' Sort and Display Preferences

While you're here in the Mail, Contacts, Calendars preferences, you have the option to change the sort order used in organizing your contacts. The Sort Order preference determines how Contacts alphabetizes contacts in the list view (left side) of your address book.

The Display Order preference determines how the name on an individual card is displayed.

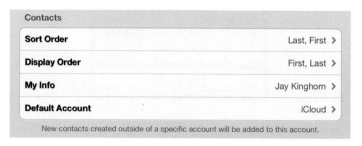

Stay on Top of Your To-Do List with Reminders

Rounding out a trio of built-in productivity apps is Reminders, a handy to-do list that is integrated with the iPad's Notification Center and your iCal or Microsoft Outlook calendar quite effectively. In this section, I'll show you how Reminders is a powerful tool that you'll find indispensable.

Power Through Your To-Do List

I'm a big fan of David Allen's "Getting Things Done" methodology for time management and productivity. One of the cornerstones to this approach is having a place to "remember" all the tidbits of information you have to keep track of. Reminders can be used to store this valuable information for you, particularly if you have an iPhone, as you'll always have one of these devices with you to capture your to-dos. iCloud synchronizes your reminders between devices, so you'll have a place to record your thoughts as well as a convenient place to view all your upcoming tasks.

Figure 6-3 shows Reminders' main window with a listing of all your to-do lists on the left and the individual items for the currently selected list on the right.

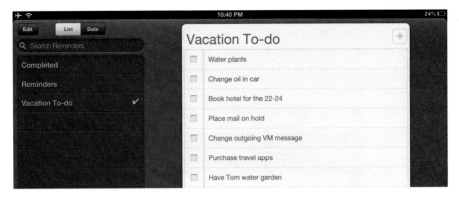

Figure 6-3   *Reminders helps you keep track of all the items on your to-do list.*

To create a new to-do item on the current list, tap the + button in the upper-right corner of the screen, or tap and hold a blank line of the to-do list. The onscreen keyboard will appear for you to type the contents of your new item.

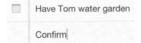

Tap the Close Keyboard button to complete typing and close the onscreen keyboard, or tap the RETURN key to jump to the next line and enter another item.

As you complete the items on your list, tap the blank square to the left of the to-do item to mark the item completed with a check mark. Completed items remain in the list for a brief period of time before they are moved to the Completed Items list.

Modify Details for aTo-Do

Tap a to-do item to add details, make changes, or delete an item entirely. In the Details pop-up menu, tap in the item heading to make a change, and tap the Reminder heading to set a reminder for a specific date and time. Swipe to move the On A Day switch from Off to On, and then specify when you'd like to be reminded to complete the to-do item. Tap the Show More heading in the bottom of the Details pop-up menu to reveal additional fields. For example, you can move the to-do item to a different list or add a note, like a phone number or address.

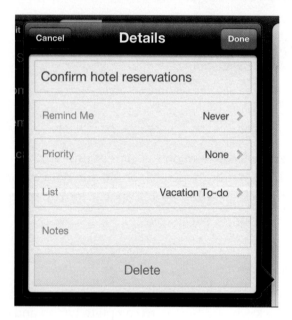

At the bottom of the Details menu is a Delete button for erasing your to-do item from the list. Tap Done when you're finished editing your to-do item.

Add or Remove Reminders Lists

The column on the left side of the screen displays all your to-do lists as well as the Completed list, which automatically displays all completed items. Should you need to move an item off the Completed list, simply tap the check mark to remove it and it will be quickly restored to the original to-do list.

To remove or rename a to-do list, tap the Edit button in the upper-left corner of the screen. Tap the red circle with the white dash inside to reveal the Delete button for removing lists, and associated to-do's, from the Reminders app.

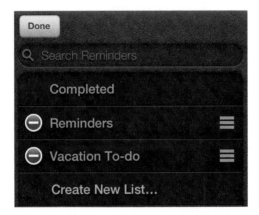

Use the three horizontal bars to the right of an item to drag it to a new position on the list, or tap Create A New List to create a new list. A blue cursor will appear within the heading for you to title your list using the onscreen keyboard.

Tap Done in the upper-left corner when you're finished editing your lists.

Search Reminders

As your lists grow, you may need to search for a specific to-do item. Use the Search tab located at the top of the left side of the screen. As you type, Reminders will filter and display to-do items matching your search criteria.

Reminders and Notification Center

As a final reminder Notification Center serves to display all the information that is relevant to you right now. As a result, Notification Center only displays items from your reminder list with reminders for today or previous days.

In the Notifications window, past-due items have a small alarm icon next to them, while items that have not reached their due date do not. Finally, you can specify the number of items displayed in the Reminders portion of your Notifications window within the Notifications preferences heading in the Settings app.

Calendars, Contacts, and Reminders are three apps that are great at helping you manage and keep up with your busy life. In the next chapter, I'll shift focus to working with a larger array of apps, both those created by Apple and from third-party developers.

7

Explore, Install, and Organize Apps

In my opinion, the brilliance of the iPad lies not solely in the elegant hardware or the collection of Apple-created apps that ship with your iPad. Instead, I believe the most remarkable feature of the iPad is the way it has become an innovative platform for outside software developers to build apps—hundreds of thousands of them—that allow you to do far more with your iPad than one could imagine. To get the most out of your iPad, you must explore this universe of apps. If you don't, it's like buying a brand-new sports car and driving it gingerly around a parking lot—with the emergency brake on.

The App Store is your portal to finding and acquiring new apps for your iPad and delivering you updates as new versions of your apps become available. So, I'll start the chapter there, at the App Store, and later I'll give you techniques for managing and organizing your apps and help you transfer files between your iPad and your computer using iTunes, iCloud, and other online services. Along the way, I'll point out five of my favorite "must-have" apps for you to begin building your app collection.

Welcome to the App Store

The App Store is an ever-growing clearinghouse of apps for your iPad, the iPhone, and iPod touch. Every app in the App Store has been reviewed by Apple to ensure they are "reliable, perform as expected, and are free of explicit and offensive material." This review process should give you confidence that the apps you purchase and download from the App Store will be free from any viruses, malware, or offensive content and will not disrupt other, previously installed apps on your iPad.

Find Apps in the App Store

You can access the App Store either from your iPad or from your computer. With either device, you'll need an active Internet connection and the Apple ID user name and password used when you set up your iPad. Your Apple ID links your purchases and downloads with your Apple ID account and allows you to install your app on all your devices, and makes it easy to recover an app in case it is deleted accidentally.

On your iPad, tap the App Store icon to access the App Store.

On your computer, launch the iTunes application. In the left column, click the iTunes Store heading. Then, when the iTunes Store loads, click the App Store heading near the top of the screen. If you're presented with the option, click the iPad heading. This ensures you're looking only at apps for the iPad, not any other types of content available through the iTunes Store.

Even though the layout and organization of the App Store differ between your iPad's App Store and iTunes on your computer, the apps contained in each version of the App Store are identical. For simplicity's sake, I'll describe the features and use of the App Store on your iPad.

To begin your tour of the App Store on your iPad, tap the blue App Store icon on your Home screen and then tap the Featured icon from the tab bar at the bottom of the screen. The Featured page highlights the best new apps for your iPad, is updated regularly, and is a great resource for finding new apps as they are released. At the top of the page are three headings:

- **New**   Contains the New and Noteworthy selections along with the iPad Game and App of the Week—high-quality apps hand-picked by Apple's staff for your enjoyment.

- **What's Hot**   An aggregate of the most downloaded apps from the App Store along with apps selected for their relevancy to current events. For example, the Summer at the Movies group of apps help you find the best summer blockbuster.

- **Release Date**   A listing of the newest apps in the App Store, sorted alphabetically. While these apps are the freshest in the App Store, most don't yet have any user reviews so they may be a bit of a gamble in terms of quality and ease of use. In the upper-right corner, you will see the option to sort by app name, most popular, and release date.

Purchase and Download Apps

To the right of an app's icon, below the title, you'll find category information to help you quickly gather the purpose, or focus, of the app, the date the app was added to the App Store or the date of the most recent update, and, if the app has been reviewed, the app's star rating. Users are able to rate apps on a scale of one to five stars, with five stars indicating a superlative app.

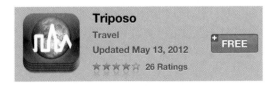

To the right of this information is a gray rectangle listing of the app's price, where you'll often see a small plus symbol (+). This indicates the app is designed for both the iPad and iPhone. These hybrid apps, as they are called, offer greater value if you own an iPhone or iPod touch as well, as the app can be used on all these devices.

To purchase an app, tap the app's price. The price field will switch to "Install App" for free apps or "Buy App" for paid apps. Tap a second time to confirm your selection and, if prompted, enter the password for your Apple ID to begin downloading the app. If you're purchasing a paid app, the purchase price, plus applicable taxes, will be charged to the credit card on file with your Apple ID account or the remaining balance on a gift card.

Free vs. Paid Apps

Building a great app takes a team of designers and programmers to transform an initial concept into a fully functioning app that stimulates your imagination and makes your life easier or more fun. This process doesn't come cheaply. As a result, I'm seeing a trend toward paid apps and an increase in the overall quality of apps.

Even free apps come with subsequent costs. Often, they are limited in functionality and serve more as a trial version of the full app or encourage you to purchase additional modules within the app. And, just like with TV and radio, advertising can be a means to subsidize free content. Many free apps have ads interspersed with the content or embedded into the app window.

Given that most paid apps cost less than five dollars, I encourage you to search both the paid and free apps as you're developing your app library, as they are often a great value for the money and make your iPad experience more rewarding. In this book, I'll highlight both free and paid apps that I feel help you to get the most out of your iPad. For the paid apps, I emphasize apps I feel have excellent quality and value relative to their cost.

Learn More About an App

To learn more about an app before you purchase it, tap the app's icon to go to the app's information page. Along the left column of the page, you'll find the app's price category and language information along with the app's parental rating. Below the parental rating, you'll find information about the app's compatibility with older iPads and iOS operating systems, as well as other devices the app can be used on.

Category: Travel
Updated: May 13, 2012
Version: 1.7.3
Size: 21.9 MB
Language: English
Seller: Triposo Inc
© Triposo

Rated 12+ for the following:

• Infrequent/Mild Alcohol, Tobacco, or Drug Use or References

Requirements:
Compatible with iPhone, iPod touch, and iPad.
Requires iOS 4.3 or later.

Farther down the column on the left side are two buttons to direct you to the developer's website and an app support page. Should you run into any problems with your app, these are great resources for troubleshooting the app or contacting the developer directly.

Also listed in this column are the most common in-app purchases. This is additional functionality or content that can be purchased from within the app. For example, a recipe app may have additional volumes of recipes available for purchase, or a game may allow you to purchase more powerful weapons or additional levels for a fee.

Along the right side of the app's information page is a description of the app, screen shots of the app, and customer ratings, which can be a good guide to the quality of the app. Tap the More heading to the right of the description to read a longer description of the app and its features. Take note of whether the app description indicates it has been updated for the higher-resolution Retina display of your third-generation iPad. Apps designed for the Retina display appear much crisper and visually more stunning than apps designed for older models.

If you'd like to preview additional screen shots from the app, swipe from right to left to reveal additional images of the app's interface and design.

To download or purchase an app from the app's information screen, tap the app's price immediately below the icon. Tap a second time to confirm your selection; then, if prompted, enter your Apple ID password to begin the download process.

 The App Store only allows apps larger than 50MB to be downloaded via Wi-Fi connection or from your computer, not with a cellular data connection on your Wi-Fi + Cellular iPad.

Understand Parental Ratings in the App Store

The App Store and iTunes Store provide a rating system, much like the rating systems used on TV and for Hollywood movies, to provide parents the opportunity to choose which apps are appropriate for their children. They also help adult users understand what types of content an app contains, so they can decide whether they may enjoy the app. Each app's information page lists the type of content a parent should be aware of. For more information on Apple's app ratings and what they mean, visit http://ipad.about.com/od/iPad_Games/a/iPad-Parental-Ratings-Explained.htm.

You can review the rating criteria by clicking an app's rating from within the iTunes App Store on your computer.

As a reminder, you are able to restrict access to applications, or types of content, within the Settings | General | Restrictions heading.

 Restricted apps will not appear on your iPad's Home screen. They will appear in your Updates and Purchased Items menus; however, the download buttons will be grayed out, preventing a user from downloading the app. Should you find you're having trouble installing updates or downloading deleted apps, you may need to first disable Restrictions to complete your download.

Search for Specific Apps

If you know exactly which app you're looking for, you can search for apps by name or subject by typing in the Search box in the upper-right corner of any tab within the App Store, except Updates. Your search

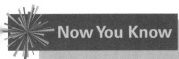

Now You Know   **iPhone Apps on Your iPad**

If you come across an iPhone app that has not yet been redesigned as an iPad app, you can still install and run it. When you open the app, it will play using the native resolution of the iPhone. Tap the 2x button, toward the bottom of the screen, to enlarge the app's window to fill the screen on your iPad. The app will run normally, but the graphics and text are often very fuzzy. For that reason, it's best to use apps designed for the iPad whenever possible.

results will be displayed in a split screen, with iPad apps listed on top and iPhone apps on the bottom.

Review the Best Sellers

Tap the Top Charts icon in the black tab bar along the bottom of the App Store window to display a list of the most popular free and paid iPad apps. The next icon, Categories, displays apps according to the category of their usage. I find this search method to be more effective for finding a particular type of app, as the Categories view will show you the most popular apps within a given category, like entertainment or education.

Purchase Apps with a Redeem Code or Gift Card

A redeem code allows you to download an app free of charge. Starbucks' App of the Week promotion is a good example, offering customers cards with redemption codes found at the pick-up counter of participating stores. To use a code and download your free app, scroll to the bottom of any window, except Updates, and tap the Redeem button. Use the onscreen keyboard to type your redemption code in the Code field. If prompted, reenter your Apple ID and password to download your app.

Follow the same steps to apply credit from a gift card to your Apple ID account. Your account balance is displayed within the Redeem Window and can also be accessed by tapping the Apple ID heading at the bottom of any window, except Updates. In the alert that appears, tap View Apple ID, then reenter your Apple ID password, and your balance will be displayed at the top of your Account Settings window.

Let Genius Recommend New Apps

A great way to discover new apps, the Genius Recommendations for Apps feature, accessed from the Genius icon in the black tab bar, will review your installed apps and recommend additional apps that you may like.

At the top of the Genius window you'll also notice a tab labeled iPad Upgrades. This shows additional versions of apps you currently have installed. If you have a free version of an alarm clock app with limited functions, for instance, the Upgrades window will show you the available full version of the app.

Update Your Apps

Periodically, app developers release free updates to add new features, improve an app's graphics, and fix software bugs. The App Store tracks the release of new updates and notifies you when upgrades are available. You can update your apps either through the App Store on your iPad or with iTunes on your computer.

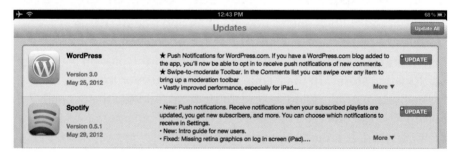

To update apps within the App Store on your iPad:

1. Tap the App Store icon to launch the App Store.
2. Tap the Updates icon from the tab bar at the bottom of the screen.
3. Tap the Update button to update a specific app or Update All to download and install all available updates.
4. Enter your password to begin the download and installation process.

If your apps contain age-restricted material, you may receive an alert reminding you of the app's age status. If you've enabled restrictions on the types of apps that can be used on the iPad, updates to apps affected by those restrictions will be grayed out and cannot be updated.

To update apps from iTunes on your computer:

1. Launch iTunes and click the Apps heading in the left column of options.
2. In the lower-right corner of the window showing all your apps, click the heading <*N*> Updates Available. This will take you to the updates page in the iTunes Store.
3. In the upper-right corner of the My App Updates screen, click Download All Free Updates.
4. Enter your Apple ID password to download updates. These updates will be installed the next time you connect your iPad to your computer with the USB cable and perform an iTunes sync.

Downloading Apps

While apps are downloading, you can continue to use your iPad normally. Apps being upgraded will continue to download then install the updates in the background while you work. An app in the process of being upgraded cannot be used until the update is complete.

Should you need to pause the update process for an app, tap the app's icon on your Home screen. The progress heading below the app icon will change from "Loading" to "Paused." Tap the app icon a second time to resume the download and installation process.

Reinstall Apps

If your download is interrupted by a slow or dropped Internet connection, the app should resume the download automatically. On occasion, this causes an error in the app's installation and prevents the app from working correctly. Should this occur, you'll need to delete the corrupted app from your iPad and then reinstall it from the App Store. Be sure you're on a Wi-Fi connection to download apps larger than 50MB.

1. From your Home screen, tap and hold the app's icon to make the icons on the page jiggle.

2. Tap the "X" in the upper-left corner of the corrupted app to delete it. In the alert that appears, confirm that you wish to delete the app by tapping Delete.

3. Tap the Home button to stop your apps from jiggling.

4. Launch the App Store app and tap the Purchased icon in the tab bar.

5. Locate the app within your list of purchased apps. To make this process easier, tap the Not On This iPad heading at the top of the screen or use the search bar to search for a specific title.

6. Tap the Cloud icon to download and install a fresh copy of your app. For paid apps, you may be directed to a second screen within the App Store where you can access the Install button.

You can also recover apps you've deleted, either to save space or because you didn't find the app to be a valuable addition to your iPad at the time. Follow steps 4–6 listed previously to download your app again from the App Store.

Share Apps with All Your Devices

If you have more than one iPad, or have other members of the Apple mobile device family (iPhone, iPod touch), you can automatically download your purchased apps, iTunes music, and iBooks to other devices associated with your Apple ID.

Go to the Settings app on your other iOS device (iPhone, iPod touch, etc.) and tap the Store heading. In the Automatic Downloads section, slide the switches to "On" for the types of content you'd like to have automatically downloaded to your other devices. When your other devices are active and connected to a Wi-Fi network, they'll automatically download new apps, making it even easier to ensure your apps are up to date on all your devices.

 If you'd like your apps to download automatically using a cellular data connection, be sure to enable the Use Cellular Data preference below the Automatic Downloads heading. This will allow apps smaller than 50MB in size to begin downloading with a cellular connection. Larger apps still require a Wi-Fi connection.

Make In-app Purchases

Many apps allow you to purchase additional content, like new paintbrushes in a drawing app, more powerful weapons in a game, or new chapters in an interactive book, from within the app itself.

To make an in-app purchase, tap the icon, heading, or button within the app used to indicate your ability to make an in-app purchase. (This will vary from app to app based on design and layout.) Next, you'll see an alert confirming your intent to make a purchase and a second alert to enter your Apple ID password. Once the purchase is completed, your additional content will be made available from within the app.

You can disable in-app purchases from within the Settings app (Settings | General | Restrictions | In-App Purchases).

Five Apps to Download Right Now

Now that you know how to download and install apps, I wanted to give you a list of five of my "must have" apps. These starter apps are all free (Hooray!) and will help you to be more productive, better informed, and inspired to explore your world.

Dropbox   This free file-sharing service for Mac, PC, and mobile devices is an indispensible tool for working collaboratively, sharing photos with family members, and easily distributing files to other Internet users. The Dropbox iPad app provides access to files stored within your Dropbox account and serves as a quick and effective way of transferring files between your iPad and your computer.

Head over to the App Store to download the Dropbox app; then, use the app to create your free Dropbox account with 2GB of storage. I recommend downloading the free desktop application for your computer as well to unlock Dropbox's full potential.

Evernote   The creators of Evernote have a lofty goal—to ensure you never forget any of your important information. Use your Evernote account to clip portions of webpages you wish to read later, store your favorite recipes, or create an ever-expanding collection of photographs taken with your iPad. All this content is stored within your Evernote account where it is searchable, sharable, and easily retrieved from any of your devices.

Your basic account is free and covers the needs of most Evernote users. For Evernote power users, of which there is a growing, and vocal, number, paid accounts allow for more storage and offline access to your notebooks and options to collaborate with other Evernote users in a single notebook.

Flipboard   What would happen if all your friends sent you the best content they find online? That is what Flipboard is about. By linking Flipboard with your social media accounts, it will automatically create a customized online magazine based on the links and other content members of your social network are sharing and commenting on. Flipboard also allows you to subscribe to other "channels" covering technology, photography, the arts, sports, and entertainment to see what the Internet is talking about right now.

Wikipanion   Where is the country of Eritrea? What's the difference between RNA and DNA? This app provides access to the most comprehensive encyclopedia on the planet, Wikipedia. The Wikipanion app makes it easy to find information on virtually any topic and serves as a valuable reference tool for staying informed and remembering all those things you've long since forgotten since high school.

TED   The TED app aggregates videos from the TED (Technology, Entertainment, Design) series of conferences. Entertaining, inspiring, and enlightening, TED talks will broaden your perspectives on the world.

   Keep your eyes out for mentions of these apps later in the book, as I'll highlight ways they can make your iPad experience more fulfilling and fruitful.

Become App-Savvy

Now that you know the basics of working in the App Store and have even installed a few apps, it's time for an app workout. First, I'll take you through a warm-up routine of organizing the apps on your iPad so you can find your favorites quickly and ensure those seldom-used apps don't get lost in the crowd. Next, I'll break down the navigational and design conventions used in most apps to help you quickly acquaint yourself with any new app you add to your iPad. To give you a productivity boost, I'll teach you to become a multitasking master on the iPad by tapping, swiping, and dragging your way between apps to work and play more effectively. Then, as a finale, I'll introduce you to several ways of swapping files between your computer and your iPad.

Organize Your Apps

As you download apps to your iPad, they are added to Home screens, the orderly arrangement of apps that serves as your jumping-off point to access individual apps. At the bottom of each Home screen, a series of light dots indicates the number of Home screens. The lightest dot indicates your current location on the list.

To move between Home screens, swipe to the left or right, or tap the dots to page left or right to another screen. To quickly return to the primary Home screen, tap the Home button.

When you amass several pages of apps, it can become tedious to find a specific app when you want to use it. There are several techniques for organizing your apps to keep you working, and playing, efficiently on your iPad.

To modify the layout of apps on your iPad:

1. Tap and hold any app icon on your Home screen. This causes the app icons to jiggle, indicating they're released from the organizational grid and ready to be moved.

2. Drag an app icon to a new location on the grid, or drag and hold the app at the edge of a screen to move it to an adjacent screen.

3. Tap the Home button to save your new layout.

I find it helpful to group apps by general use. For example, I'll have a screen of games, another for work-related apps, a third for entertainment, and a fourth for reference or educational apps.

Nest Your Apps in Folders

If, after grouping, you find you still have too many apps to fit on a page, or if you've reached the maximum of 11 Home pages on your iPad, you can nest up to 20 apps together in folders. This serves as a logical tool for grouping specific apps together, like photography or social media, and helps organize your Home screens.

Nest apps together as follows:

1. Release your apps from the grid using the tap and hold method outlined previously.

2. Drag one app icon on top of another until a dark gray outline appears around the pairing.

3. The nested apps will appear in a row together and other apps will be ghosted to white. The folder will automatically be named according to the category of the apps.

4. Tap the folder name to change or modify it.

5. Tap outside the nested row of apps to add more apps to your folder.

6. Tap the Home button to save your new arrangement.

You can easily modify the contents or name of the folder by causing the apps to jiggle and then tapping the folder icon on the Home screen. The row of apps is revealed, allowing you to

- Drag items out of the folder to remove them from the folder

- Adjust the order of apps within the folder

- Rename the folder

To delete a folder, drag all the contents out of the folder and the folder will be deleted automatically.

Tap the Home button to save the contents of your folder.

Place Your Favorite Apps in the Dock

The Dock, located at the bottom of your Home screens, is a convenient way of storing up to six of your most commonly used apps. Because the Dock is visible on all Home screens, you know you can always access these apps without the need to hunt for the app's icon or to swipe through several screens.

To add items to the Dock, tap and hold an app icon until the apps jiggle and then drag an app onto an open space in the Dock. To remove an app from the Dock, drag it onto an open space on a Home screen.

 Add a folder of apps to the Dock to give you quick access to a group of apps. This allows you to have access to more than the Dock's six-app limit.

Delete Unused Apps

Clean up the clutter on your Home screens by deleting apps you never use. When the apps jiggle on your Home screen, tap the black-and-white "X" in the upper-left corner of the app icon. Confirm the deletion in the Alert box that appears.

Should you later change your mind, you can always download deleted apps again using the steps outlined in the "Reinstall Apps" section earlier in the chapter.

 The base set of apps, like the App Store, Mail, and Calendars, that come pre-installed on your iPad, cannot be deleted.

Use iTunes to Organize Your Apps

You can also organize apps within the iTunes app on your computer. When your iPad is connected to your computer with the USB cable:

1. Click your iPad's listing beneath the Devices heading on the left column of the screen.

2. Click the Apps heading near the top of the screen to display your list of apps.

3. Use your mouse to drag, arrange, and nest apps as described previously.

Multitask on the iPad

The iPad allows you to work with more than one app at a time so you can stream music from an Internet radio app, like Pandora, while sorting through your Inbox in the Mail app. This section will help you become a multitasking ninja so you can quickly jump between apps with ease.

Access the Multitasking Bar

To see which apps are currently open, double-tap the Home button from any screen. The current display slides up to reveal the multitasking bar and shows all apps currently running in the background. Tap another app's icon to jump to that app. There's no need to "quit" or "exit" out of your current app first. Apps not in use go into a "suspended" state if they are not performing a task like playing music.

Use Multitasking Gestures

A small collection of gestures allows you to jump between apps or quickly return to the main Home screen. Think of these as a secret handshake for iPad multitasking masters.

First, be sure Multitasking Gestures is enabled from the General preferences within the Settings app. The text below the preference provides a handy reference for the following gestures:

- **Four-finger swipe (left or right)** The four-finger swipe allows you to move between apps almost as though they were stacked on top of one another. Place four or five fingers on the center of the screen. Drag to the left or right to scroll between open apps.

- **Four-finger swipe (up)** Use four fingers and swipe up to reveal the multitasking bar, to close unneeded apps, or to jump to another app.

- **Four-finger pinch** Use four or five fingers in a closing pinch to jump from an app to the Home screen without using the Home button.

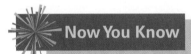

Now You Know **Exit Apps to Free Up Memory**

Periodically, it is a good idea to close open apps to free up your iPad's memory and make the apps you're actively using more responsive. To do this, double-tap to reveal all open apps, and then tap and hold an app's icon for three seconds. The app icons will begin to jiggle, just like when you reorganized apps earlier in this chapter. You will also see a small red circle with a dash in the upper-left corner of the icons. Tap this circle to close an app. This is a great way to restore your iPad's performance should it start to feel sluggish, and is an effective troubleshooting technique in case you begin to experience apps crashing unexpectedly.

You can also double-tap the Home button to quickly access the player controls for the Music app or to adjust the brightness of your screen. When the row of background apps appears, swipe to scroll left to the player controls. Tap outside the multitasking bar to close it and return to your previous app.

Transfer Files Between Your iPad and Your Computer

By and large, working on the iPad is an intuitive, elegant experience. However, there are a few rough edges, like transferring files, that don't live up to one's expectations. As I mentioned in the beginning of the book, the iPad really isn't designed to work with files, and, perhaps as a result, the file transfer system built into iTunes on your computer is clunky. Fortunately, there are third-party apps that can help make the process a little smoother.

Transfer Files Using iTunes on Your Computer

To transfer files via iTunes, connect your iPad to your computer with the USB cable, launch the iTunes application on your computer, and follow these steps:

1. Click your iPad's name in the Devices heading on the left side of the iTunes window.

2. Click the Apps heading along the top of the screen, and scroll down to reveal the File Sharing heading.

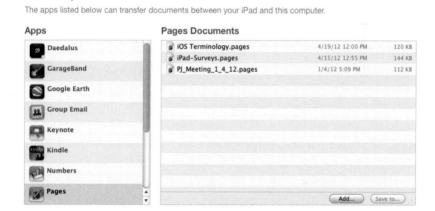

The Apps column on the left side of the File Sharing heading displays a list of all the apps that can send and/or receive files through iTunes. To transfer a file from your computer to your iPad:

1. Click the app's heading and press Add to select a file using your computer's operating system window.

2. To open the file on your iPad, launch the app you've targeted in the previous step. Click the + icon, and select iTunes from the pop-up menu. In the second pop-up menu, you'll see a list of available files from iTunes. Tap the file to copy it to your application.

To send files from your applications to your computer via iTunes:

1. Open the document on your iPad in the appropriate app.

2. In Apple iWork apps, tap the wrench icon to open the Share And Print pop-up menu. In other apps, tap the Action Item icon to open your sharing or export options.

3. Tap Send To iTunes.

4. In iTunes, click your app in the File Sharing window. In the right column, you'll see a list of available documents. Click the document you wish to transfer.

5. Click the Save To button to save your file to your computer's hard drive.

This system works best with Apple-created apps that can send and receive files in both directions. Unfortunately, not all apps can. Apps that appear in the File Sharing window on iTunes often only have one-directional support for file transfers. The Kindle app, for example, will automatically import any PDF files added to the File Sharing window. There is no icon or way for you to know which type of sharing is supported by the app other than to experiment.

My recommendation is to use iTunes for sharing files in and out of Apple-created apps like Keynote, Pages, Garage Band, and Numbers.

What About the Other Options in the Share And Print Menu?

In the Share And Print pop-up menu found within your Apple apps like Pages and Keynote, there are several other options for sharing your files. In addition to iTunes, Print, and Email, there are options to Share Via iWork.com, Copy To iDisk, and Copy To WebDAV. Unfortunately, Apple is no longer supporting two of the options (iWork.com and iDisk), and WebDAV could be a great option for sharing files, particularly between an iPad and a Mac computer, but the technical skills required to set up the WebDAV account correctly place it well out of the scope of this book.

Three Better Ways of Sharing Files

Since the iPad's file-sharing capabilities are a bit clunky, I want to highlight easier ways to share files between your computer and your iPad. These options are simpler and supported in a wider number of apps:

- **Email**   Many apps allow you to share your file as an e-mail attachment for a quick means of sending files from your iPad to your computer. You've already learned ways to open attached files into apps on your iPad. For a review, visit Chapter 5.

- **Dropbox**   The web-based, file-sharing application Dropbox is my favorite option for sharing files quickly between my computer and iPad. With the Dropbox app installed on my iPad, I drop files from my computer into my Dropbox folders; then launch the Dropbox app on my iPad and browse files in the shared folder. From Dropbox, I can open files in their respective apps, create public links to shared items, or delete items in Dropbox I no longer need access to.

- **Evernote**   I've already mentioned Evernote as a tool for storing bits of information you encounter online or in person, but did you know that Evernote can also store and transfer documents? When the Evernote app is installed on your iPad, you can send documents from many apps on your iPad directly to your Evernote account. Use Evernote over Dropbox when you want files to be searched from within your Evernote account— handwritten notes, for example. Files can be tricky to get out of Evernote, so if file sharing is your primary concern, Dropbox is a better option.

As you've seen from this chapter, the iPad offers many opportunities to organize your life. In following chapters, I'll give you insight into more apps that you can use to entertain, educate, and inform yourself.

8

Your Mobile Entertainment Center

Your iPad is ideally suited to be your portable entertainment center with dozens of options to watch TV shows, movies, and videos; listen to music; or unwind with a game built for the dazzling graphics of the Retina display. In this chapter I'll walk you through the ways you can download and stream movies, videos, and music to your iPad and get your game collection started with a trio of my favorites.

Is Your iPad a Mini TV in Disguise?

It's the end of a long day and you're looking to relax on the sofa and watch your favorite TV shows. Only instead of reaching for your remote control, you reach for your iPad. There are several options for watching your "must see" TV shows on your iPad. So many, in fact, that you may just be able to ditch your cable company and watch all your television on your iPad instead of your cable box. Here's a rundown of your TV options along with some potential gotchas you might encounter should you decide to cut the cable.

Broadcast and Cable TV

Your television-watching options fall into four basic categories.

Channel-Specific Apps (ABC, NBC, PBS, HBO-Go)   A number of broadcast and cable TV stations have their own channel-specific apps. Many of these apps are free, though apps for cable TV stations, like TNT and HBO, require you to verify your cable-TV subscription before you're able to watch TV shows on your iPad.

The ABC Player app is a good example of how a television experience can be transported to the iPad. You're able to watch full episodes of popular shows like *Modern Family, Grey's Anatomy,* and *20/20* with limited commercial interruptions free of charge. They do require an Internet connection to stream episodes, which prevents you from watching on most airplane flights or long car rides. When you do have a broadband Internet connection, the picture is sharp, vibrant, and very engaging on the iPad's screen.

Although not technically a channel-specific app, the MLB At Bat app allows you to watch every Major League Baseball game outside of your home market for $27.99 a month. The app is a gold mine for baseball fans, as it includes free box scores of all the day's games, audio broadcasts, and a Gameday view, which transforms pitch-by-pitch box scores to a visually rich experience.

Subscription Apps (Hulu Plus)   If you'd prefer to have just one location for watching your favorite shows, Hulu Plus is the place to go. Aggregating TV shows from major broadcast TV and cable networks along with independent content producers, Hulu Plus offers a large library of current TV shows, classic movies, and news for you to watch on your iPad. Although you are able to use the free version of Hulu on your computer, you must purchase Hulu Plus for your iPad, for a $7.99/month subscription, via your Internet connection.

Purchase Seasons or Episodes (iTunes Store)   The iTunes app allows you to purchase single episodes or full seasons of your favorite shows, from a comprehensive offering from the "big three" networks as well as shows from Bravo, HBO, Showtime, and AMC. Individual episodes typically run around $3, while full seasons run around $30 for standard-definition episodes and $40 to 50 for high-definition episodes.

Unlike the two options listed previously, purchasing shows gives you more options because it allows you to download them to your iPad for viewing without an Internet connection.

Downloaded TV shows are watched within the Videos app on your iPad and are best managed through iTunes as described in Chapter 3.

Stream from Your Cable Box (SlingPlayer)   Slingbox is a physical piece of hardware that connects to your cable TV and makes your cable TV connection available over the Internet. It's what allows my brother-in-law to watch American basketball while living in Europe. When paired with the SlingPlayer iPad app ($29.99), Slingbox allows you to watch your TV, change channels, or schedule DVR recordings over the Internet on your iPad. The Slingbox and SlingPlayer require you to have a cable TV subscription and Internet connection for watching your favorite shows. The DVR feature allows you to watch shows at a convenient time, provided you remember to record them. For sports fans, the SlingPlayer is an ideal solution for watching your favorite team when you're away from home, as live sports are difficult, if not impossible, to watch on the iPad.

Make TV a Social Experience

An increasingly large number of TV viewers are using their iPad not only to watch TV, but also to engage in live conversation about their favorite shows with other TV watchers.

Twitter is a common platform for TV discussion. To join, use the show's name as a hashtag within your favorite Twitter app and you'll see a live feed of all discussions related to the show. This can enliven a dry political debate, start a debate of your own with other sports fans, or spur a chat about the fashions on the red carpet during the annual awards shows.

Other social TV apps, like Miso, Into_Now, and Get Glue, aim to build social communities around television shows within their apps. Currently, participation is low relative to Twitter, and therefore, less engaging.

A few TV shows have their own apps to integrate social media discussion, additional clues, and character stories along with fan polls and cast biographies. If you're a die-hard fan, have a look in the App Store to see if your favorite show has an app to give you even more of the show you love.

Bring the Big Screen to Your iPad

Your iPad can also be a source for watching Hollywood movies and independent films. Although the screen is much smaller than watching a movie in the theater, movies on your iPad's Retina display can be captivating experiences. Because you typically hold your iPad much closer to your face than you would a laptop or TV, the screen *feels* larger. Proximity, combined with the high-resolution display and a good pair of headphones, make watching movies on your iPad a great cinema experience, but it loses impact when two or more people try and watch together.

Rent or Purchase Movies from iTunes

The best selection of movies for your iPad is found in the iTunes Store. Tap the iPad app and select the Movies icon from the tab bar at the bottom of the screen to search for movies to rent or purchase.

Tap a movie thumbnail to view details about the movie, watch a preview, rent, or purchase the movie. Below the main heading, you'll find a plot summary, list of actors, and cast details about the movie, including file size, reviews from Rotten Tomatoes, and customer ratings. The file size is an important consideration, as a high-definition movie can take several hours to download completely over a standard broadband connection. You'll also need to ensure your iPad contains sufficient storage space to store the movie.

 To check available space on your iPad, exit the iTunes app and launch the Settings app. In the General heading, tap Usage and your available storage space is listed at the top of the page.

Movies can be rented in either standard- or high-definition, with the high-definition rentals, on average, a dollar more expensive. Rented movies can be downloaded to your iPad or computer, and you're allowed 30 days to begin watching your movie. Once you begin a movie, you have 24 hours to complete it before the rental expires and the movie is automatically removed from your library. Rented and purchased movies are played and managed with the Videos app.

Watch Movies in the Videos App

The Videos app is a convenient place to play back video content purchased or rented from the iTunes Store, videos you've created, or video podcasts you subscribe to using iTunes. In Chapter 3, I discussed ways you can control which types of videos are synced to your iPad and how you can transfer rented movies between your computer and iPad using the iTunes application on your computer. This section introduces you to the features and functionality of the Videos app.

When you launch the Videos app, you'll find a thumbnail display of movies you have stored on your iPad. Along the top, tabs for Movies, Podcasts, TV Shows, Music Videos, and Rentals reflect the kind of content available on your iPad. For example, the Rentals tab is hidden when you don't have any rented movies available to watch. In the upper-right corner, the Edit button allows you to delete individual movies to free up space on your iPad. Tap the Edit button, and then tap the black-and-white "X" in the upper-left corner of the movie thumbnail to delete the movie. An alert appears to make sure you really do want to delete the movie. Confirm deletion and the movie is removed from your iPad.

On the left side of the Videos window you'll find the Store button, which takes you to the Movies section of the iTunes Store where you can replenish your movie collection.

Within the Videos app, tap a movie, video podcast, or TV show thumbnail to bring up more information, reviews, and age ratings. Tap the Play button to play a movie, or tap a podcast or TV episode thumbnail to play the desired episode. If you don't want to purchase a video, you can always return to your Video app by swiping four fingers from right to left.

During playback, your video will fill the screen. To bring up your video player controls, tap briefly on the screen. At the top of the screen, a scrub bar shows the duration of the movie, the amount played, and a playhead you can drag to a new location to scrub back or forward in the video.

 When your finger is on the playhead, high-speed scrubbing allows you to move quickly through the video. When you move your finger down the screen and continue scrubbing, you'll see that the scrubbing slows to make it easier to find a specific scene to resume playback.

On the far-right side of the scrubber bar is a button to watch the video in widescreen mode (with black bars on the top and bottom) or to fill the screen (crops the right and left sides of the picture).

At the bottom of the window are your playback controls: Play/Pause, Next, and Previous buttons. Tap the Next or Previous button to jump to the next or previous chapter in a movie or tap, and hold to fast-forward or rewind the movie. If you're on a wireless network shared by an AirPlay-supported playback device, like an Apple TV, that allows you to stream your iTunes library wirelessly, the right side of the playback bar will display the AirPlay option. To use AirPlay, tap the AirPlay icon and select the device you'd like to stream the video to. It really is that easy. I watched a five-year-old use it to watch her favorite shows.

At the bottom of the player controls is the volume slider. Drag to make the video louder or quieter. You can also use the Volume switch on the side of the iPad to control playback volume, or, if you're listening with headphones, use any of the volume controls on your Apple-approved headphones to adjust volume, pause play, or move to the previous or next chapter of the movie.

When you're finished watching your movie, tap the screen to bring up the playback controls, and then tap Done in the upper-left corner to exit the player window.

Additional Movie and Video Options

If you'd prefer not to purchase movies and would like more flexible viewing than the iTunes rentals allow for, try the Netflix app. Your monthly Netflix streaming subscription allows you to view commercial-free TV shows and full-length movies. The streaming consistency is very good and playback adapts when your Internet connection fluctuates, so your movie doesn't falter or pause.

As an alternative to Netflix, check out Crackle. The selection is limited when compared to the expansive offerings from iTunes and Netflix, but the app and movies are free, albeit with commercial interruptions. A third option, SnagFilms, aims to "bring the world of independent film to broader audiences."

Independent, Amateur, and Niche Content

Continuing in the vein of independent and amateur storytelling, I would be remiss to discuss online video without mentioning YouTube. Preinstalled on your iPad, the YouTube app is a portal to viewing short-form video, amateur stunts, and, of course, lots of cat videos. The YouTube app is built around Apple's design standards, making it very easy to navigate, and is integrated well with the iPad, allowing you to upload your own creations, shot, edited, and published with your iPad.

While YouTube's video volume is staggering, I find the videos on Vimeo to be of higher artistic quality.

The Vimeo app itself is clean and easy to navigate. Surprisingly, it isn't just an app for watching movies. You can use it to shoot, edit, and upload your own creations to your Vimeo account, entirely within the app.

With plenty of video to go around—72 hours of video are uploaded just to YouTube every minute of every day—enterprising companies are creating apps to help you sort through it all. ShowYou, a video aggregation app, collects the videos creating the biggest buzz and presents them in a large mosaic, with larger videos being the most widely shared. Sign in with Twitter or Facebook to see the videos making the rounds on your social networks, or slide the grid to the left to see collections of videos from a diverse range of contributors like the Museum of Modern Art, The Colbert Report, the American Film Institute, and MIT.

Playing and Discovering Music on Your iPad

Rarely do you find me working without music playing in the background. At my desk, while writing this book, I listen to a steady stream of music both from my own library and new music from a trio of online services. Fortunately, when I'm working on my iPad away from my office, I can take my music, and music services, with me. In this section I'll help you make sure you don't miss a beat as your iPad accompanies you throughout your day.

Music, Your iTunes Library on the Go

The Music app, preinstalled on your iPad, serves as your iPad's extension of your iTunes library. In Chapter 3, I discussed ways to synchronize some, or all, of your iTunes music collection to your iPad. Once you've copied the songs over to your iPad, the fun begins. The Music app is designed to be a touch-friendly music experience, with your artists and albums arranged in a colorful grid. Along the top, you'll find playback controls nestled in the top-left corner with a volume slider in the top-right corner.

The center of the top control bar displays the song, artist, and album with controls to repeat or shuffle songs. Along the right side of this section, you'll find the Genius logo. Tap the logo for the iTunes Genius service to automatically create a playlist of songs from your library based on your current selection. Unfortunately, there is no visible clue that your playlist has been created. You have to go to the Playlist heading located at the bottom of the screen to see your Genius Playlist and the songs it's selected for you. Additional tabs along the bottom of the window allow you to sort your collection by playlist, song, artist, or album. The More tab provides access to additional genres of content, like podcasts, and gives you the option to sort by music genre or composer. A Search tab located in the right corner helps you find a specific song, while the Store button in the left corner helps you purchase new tracks from the iTunes Store.

If you have your iPad connected to the same network as AirPlay-enabled speakers, like the Jawbone Jambox, you can wirelessly send music from your iPad to your speakers. To do so, tap the AirPlay icon in the upper-right corner and select your speakers from the pop-up menu. To disconnect, tap AirPlay a second time and choose your iPad's speakers from the pop-up menu.

Find New Music You'll Love with Online Music Apps

There has been a recent shift from owning your music to having a subscription to a cloud-based music collection you can listen to whenever you want, on any device you have with you. The online radio service Pandora helped to kick off this trend with its customized radio stations that learn from your preferences to help find music you'll love. Newer entries like Spotify and MOG, and their apps of the same name, offer free access to a comprehensive streaming collection on your computer and charge a monthly subscription fee for mobile access.

Ladysmith Black Mambazo
Hlala Nami
Ilembe: Honoring Shaka Zulu

Now You Know   Streaming Media: A Word of Warning for Cellular Users

This chapter has highlighted several of the ways you can bring engaging, entertaining movies, games, TV shows, and music to your iPad. All this content, particularly movie, TV, and video content, requires a lot of bandwidth to download or stream to your iPad. If you're enjoying all this content from a cellular data connection, you can easily consume your monthly data allowance in a matter of hours. So, if you're using your cellular data connection for streaming movies, music, or TV shows, be sure to keep an eye on your data limits so as not to inadvertently exceed your monthly data plan.

You can quickly check your cellular usage in Settings | Cellular Data | View Account. This window will display the amount of data you've used along with the number of days left in your billing cycle.

I prefer Pandora for listening to a genre or style of music and like the way it selects new songs to suit my tastes. Spotify and MOG are preferable when I want to listen to a specific track or album that I don't own. Both have integration with Facebook and Twitter so you can share songs on your social network and discover new artists based on your social network's music tastes. Of course, for those times when you want to hide the fact that you've been listening to Wham! all day, you can temporarily disable your social sharing.

It's All Fun and Games in Game Center

As a sophisticated gaming control with a powerful on-board processor and a beautiful touch screen, your iPad can be a riveting, white-knuckle game console just as easily as it can serve up TV shows. There are more than 35,000 games for you to choose from in the App Store. From strategic puzzles to multiplayer shooting games, contemplative classics like Scrabble or Sudoku, to arcade wonders like Mirror's Edge, there are games for every type of player.

Game Center: A Hub for Your iPad Games

The Game Center app is an integrated gaming hub for your iPad that helps you connect with other players, track your high scores, and discover new games that you'll enjoy. It can also help you connect with online friends to enjoy multiplayer games with an integrated voice chat console.

Game Center is a stand-alone app preinstalled on your iPad and, once activated, your Game Center account links your scores and online friends between individual Game Center–enabled games and the Game Center app.

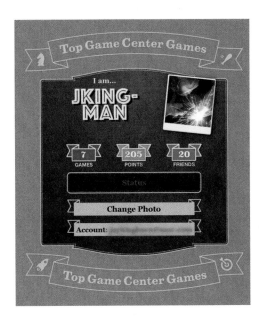

To activate or log in to Game Center:

1. Launch the Game Center app.

2. Enter your Apple ID and password, and tap Sign In. If you'd prefer not to have your Game Center account linked with your Apple ID, you can create a new account. Follow the directions onscreen to create your new account.

Once you're signed in, tap your Account heading to modify the settings. In the Account screen, you're able to adjust your privacy settings and can remove your e-mail address from the Friends listing. Tap your e-mail address in the Email heading and then tap Remove Email From Account. This will only allow friends to find you using your profile name and not your e-mail address.

On the main screen of Game Center, also called the Me screen, you can see your online gaming name, the number of games you've played, points you've accumulated ,and the number of friends you have in the Game Center network. Along the periphery of the window are icons for the most popular Game Center games. Tap any of these icons to go to the App Store to learn more about or purchase a game.

The remaining tabs along the bottom of the Game Center window are

- **Friends**   Forge new friendships over games, track the achievements of your friends, or check out the all-time leaderboards within the Friends panel. Search for friends based on Game Center's recommendations in the A–Z or Recent tab. The Points tab displays your accumulated achievement points and compares them to the world leaders. Tap the + icon to draft and send a new Game Center friend request.

  If you're having problems with a friend on Game Center, you can unfriend them from this window and, if they're being inappropriate, you can report them as a problem player.

- **Games**   The Games tab displays all the Game Center–enabled games installed on your iPad. Along the top of the window are additional game recommendations and a yellow tab below your installed games provides a quick link to the Game Center games in the App Store. Tap the game icon to see the game's info and leaderboard. From the Info window, tap Play Game to launch the game. The Achievements tab displays a listing of the game's milestones so you can track your progress toward completing a challenging new game.

 When in the App Store you can see if a game is Game Center–enabled by looking for the Game Center icon and heading below the game icon and price on the left side of the app details screen.

- **Requests**   This screen displays any pending friend requests. The yellow Add Friends tab provides another option for submitting friend requests.

Of course, there are many games for the iPad that don't use Game Center. These games track points, achievements, and player profiles independently of Game Center. Essentially, they behave like any other app on your iPad.

Three Games to Get You Started

To wrap up the discussion on games, I wanted to provide you with a selection of three games I'm enjoying right now on my iPad. These games are challenging, entertaining, and make great use of iPad's gestures for controlling the action of the game.

Contre Jour ($2.99, 4+)   My favorite game du jour is a strategic game I discovered through a Game Center recommendation. Your goal is to navigate a little creature named Petit through a land of darkness by manipulating the shape of the landscape and guiding it toward the light at the end of the level. Contre Jour is accompanied by an elegant piano soundtrack and subtle sound effects, making it a great choice for those who find rapid-paced shooter games to be overwhelming.

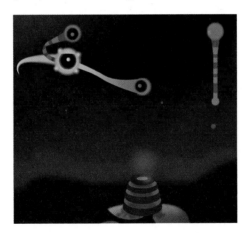

Mirror's Edge ($1.99, 9+)   You're Faith Connors, a "Runner" whose athleticism and parkour prowess allow you to leap, slide, tumble, and climb through levels to deliver sensitive messages. The game is challenging and action packed without being excessively violent or bloody. The only demerit for this game is that it hasn't yet been updated for the higher-resolution Retina display. Given the game's popularity, I expect it to be only a matter of time.

Osmos ($4.99, 4+)   In Osmos, you're a creature who is out to absorb smaller creatures into your being and gain their energy. You have to be careful—other, larger creatures want to absorb you. I'll admit, at first I found this game to be very slow. Once I made it through the first few levels, however, I found the balance of action and strategy to be just about right for my tastes. The mesmerizing graphics add to the enjoyment of the game, and I'm hoping for an update with full support for the higher-resolution Retina display. When that happens, I don't think I'll be able to tear myself away.

9

Stay Current with Books, News, and Information

Despite rapid technological advances in video streaming, on-demand TV, and interactive multimedia experiences, reading isn't likely to disappear anytime soon. It is, however, being adapted for these new mediums. The way we digest the daily news, seek out new information, and even curl up with a good book is changing. The iPad is front and center in this evolution of the printed page. From interactive e-books, textbooks, and magazines to socially curated news readers, like Flipboard and self-published blogs, e-books, and magazines that often contribute great value and perspective to cultural discussion, the written word is taking a new form—one well adapted to the strengths of the iPad.

iBooks and E-readers

The initial release of the iPad propelled the adoption and development of electronic books and helped catalyze a competition between Apple's iBooks and Amazon's Kindle for e-reader supremacy. This competition has spurred innovation and creativity on the part of publishers and tech companies, which have been greatly beneficial to consumers. In the span of only a couple of years, we've progressed from poorly formatted, text-only e-books to rich, interactive stories and textbooks complete with videos, graphics, embedded games, and audio to accompany the written word.

Text-only books have benefited as well from higher-resolution screens and brighter, sharper text that reduces eyestrain and makes it easier to read in a wide variety of environments. In addition, minimal distribution costs and improved publishing tools make it easier for independent authors to bypass traditional publishing companies and deliver their books directly to their readers.

Download and Purchase Books from the iBookstore

To begin the e-reader overview, I'll start with iBooks, a free download from the App Store and the iBooks Store, the built-in arm of the iTunes Store dedicated to filling your iBooks library with new reading material.

Tap the iBooks icon to open your iBooks library. Unless you've upgraded from a previous iPad or have begun exploring on your own, your bookshelves are probably a little bare. Tap the Store button in the upper-left corner to access the online iBookstore. By this point, the layout of the iBookstore should look familiar to you, as it mimics the design and function of both the iTunes and App Stores. One unique attribute of the iBookstore you'll notice on a book's info page is the ability to download a free sample, often the first 15 percent of the book.

Tap Download Sample to download the sample excerpt, or tap the book's price to purchase a book—much like you've done with apps, songs, or movies.

To start building your collection, tap Top Charts and swipe through the titles in the Top Free Books area to find an interesting title to download.

 The iBookstore and Kindle Bookstore have hundreds of classic novels available for free from Project Gutenberg. If you're looking to brush up on the classics of English literature or helping your child navigate their school's reading list, you can find many classic titles available here.

Before leaving the iBookstore, I want to point out the Browse tab, which allows you to search by author in both Free and Paid listings. This makes it easy to find your favorite authors, rediscover classic novels, and quickly locate a book on your reading list.

To return to your library, tap the Library button.

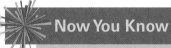 **Textbooks in the iBookstore**

Somewhat hidden from view, toward the bottom of the Categories page is the textbooks category. Here, you'll find interactive textbooks covering core topics in science, mathematics, social science, and more. These textbooks are an outstanding supplement to your child's classroom textbooks, a means of brushing up on classes long since completed, or an introduction to a new field.

Read, Annotate, and Discover iBooks

Your downloaded books and sample excerpts are displayed on your bookshelf. New titles have a blue banner over the right corner of the cover, and sample books show a red banner over the same corner.

To open an iBook, tap the cover's thumbnail on the bookshelf, and the book opens as a two-page spread when your iPad is held horizontally, or as a single page when the iPad is held vertically. A series of icons along the top of the book assist in readability, and a navigation bar along the bottom aids in navigating through the book. While reading, these tools disappear from view so as not to detract from your reading experience. To show or hide the toolbar, it's most reliable to tap in the center of the book. Should you tap in the area where the icons are located—say, the upper-right corner—you may find yourself turning the pages instead of recalling the toolbar.

 If you're reading while lying down or reclining, you'll want to enable the rotation lock. The quickest way to do so is to double-tap the Home button to open the multitasking bar and then swipe to scroll to the far-left end of the multitasking bar. To the left of the playback controls, you'll see the rotation lock button, indicated by a circular arrow. Tap it to temporarily lock rotation in the current orientation. If, instead of the rotation lock button, you see a volume button, activate rotation lock by sliding the Silent switch, located on the right side just above the volume controls.

Layout of the iBook Window

Here's a quick rundown on the functions of each icon in the iBook window, described clockwise beginning with the group of items in the top-right corner of the book. The icons present in this area will vary depending on whether you're reading a traditional or interactive e-book.

Type (Traditional E-book)   Within the Type pop-up menu, you're able to modify screen brightness, increase or decrease the size of the type on the page, select an alternate typeface for the book, or choose from one of three reading themes. An additional feature hidden from view, unless you tap the Theme button, allows you to remove the book design from the edges of the window and make your pages fill the screen.

Audio Narration   When available, the Audio Narration option begins or pauses the accompanying audio track, adjusts volume, and allows you to specify whether you'd like pages turned manually or automatically.

Brightness   This option controls the brightness of the screen with a pop-up slider.

Search   The magnifying glass opens a search field within a small pop-up menu. This allows you to quickly jump to a specific page or chapter heading and search for a specific word or phrase within the text of the book. Type in your search terms, and a list of the number of times those terms appear in the book will be displayed. Tap any of the search results to jump directly to the corresponding page. At the bottom of the menu are buttons to search for a word or phrase from your book on the Web or within Wikipedia.

Bookmarks   Like a dog-eared page in a traditional book, bookmarks serve as location reminders for important content within the book. Tap the Bookmark icon to add a bookmark. Tap a second time to remove it. You don't need to add a bookmark to indicate where you've left off in the book—iBooks will do that for you automatically. Shortly, I'll show you how to view a list of all your bookmarked and highlighted pages.

Navigation Bar   Along the bottom of the screen is a bar to quickly scan through the book. In traditional e-books, a series of dots with a slender slider allows you to drag through the text of the book. As you drag your finger, a pop-up displays the chapter and page number of the slider's new location in the book. For interactive books, small thumbnails of each page are displayed along with a light white rectangle to mark your current location. As you drag your finger, a pop-up with larger thumbnails of the page is used to preview your new location. Note that textbooks do not always have a navigation bar at the bottom of the screen.

Below the navigation bar on the right side of the screen is a display showing the number of pages remaining in the chapter. As someone who always likes to pause reading at a natural break in the material, I find this to be a valuable piece of information.

Contents   In the upper-left corner of the screen, the button with three horizontal lines provides quick access to a book's table of contents. For traditionally structured books, you'll see two additional headings at the top of the book's listing of contents: Bookmarks and Notes. Both display annotations you've made in the book. The Notes heading displays highlighted content and notes you've made relating to the book's content. In the top-right corner, the Action icon allows you to e-mail or print notes you've created. To return to your current place in the book, tap Resume.

For interactive books, the Contents button displays the pages of the book as a grid of thumbnails. Tap a page's thumbnail to jump to the page. Within the Contents window, a second icon, Bookmarks, is displayed in the upper-right corner of the window to provide access to bookmarked pages.

Textbooks separate the table of contents from the Notes section and follow common navigational conventions for working with nested content.

Buy (Samples Only)   If you're reading a sample book, the Buy button links directly to the last page of the sample chapter where you can complete your purchase and download the rest of the book.

Library   This option closes the e-book and returns you to your bookshelf to select another book.

Read, Take Notes, and Define Uncommon Words

As you'd expect from the iPad, reading an iBook uses common gestures to turn pages, highlight content, create notes, and define unfamiliar terms. The most common of all e-book tasks is, of course, turning pages. Swipe to turn to the previous or next page. If you're reading a book with accompanying audio narration, when the narration reaches the end of the page, the corner of the page will curl slightly, serving as a visual cue that it is time to turn to the next page.

The primary advantage of electronic books over paper books is the way electronic tools make it easy to discover more about the content, themes, or phrases in the book and to mark up the book with your own thoughts, notes, and highlights and then e-mail them for later reference.

When you encounter an unfamiliar word or term used in the book, double-tap the word to select it and reveal a slender pop-up menu. Tap the Define button to display a definition of the word with additional links to the Web and Wikipedia. Tap to hide this menu and return to reading.

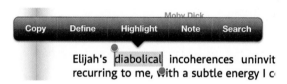

This double-tap can also be used to highlight or copy the word, phrase, or section of text for future use; create a note; or search within the text for additional instances of the selection. The Notes feature is particularly valuable when reading books for education or business, as these notes can be e-mailed for use in term papers and reports or combined with other materials.

 If you find a fact in a book you need to remember, copy the text and then create a note associated with the place in the text. When you've completed the book, e-mail notes to your Evernote account to be searched and retrieved easily. For details on setting up your Evernote e-mail account, see http://evernote.com/trunk/items/evernote-email?lang= en&layout=default.

Engage with Graphics and Interactive Elements

An increasing number of e-books contain photos, graphics, videos, and other interactive elements to illuminate a complex subject or provide deeper insight into the material. Interactive books play to the strength of electronic publishing and the iPad and, I believe, point toward the rich media we will all use to engage our senses and learn more efficiently and effectively.

When you encounter interactive elements, your instinct should be to tap them. Double-tap to enlarge photos, isolating them from the text on the page. Pinch to zoom in and view details of the photo. In most books, tap outside the photo to return to the text layout. In textbooks, tap the white "X" in the upper-left corner to return to reading.

When you encounter embedded photo slideshows or videos, tap the play button to play the video. For a slideshow of images, indicated with a series of dots below the photo or photo's caption, swipe to view additional images. In many interactive children's books, half of the joy is finding all the hidden interactivity within the book. Tap, swipe, pinch, and flick the elements you suspect contain hidden actions and see what happens!

Organize Your Bookshelf

In time, your iBook app's bookshelf can become cluttered with completed books, free book samples, and books waiting to be read. Create and use collections to tidy up your bookshelf and stay organized.

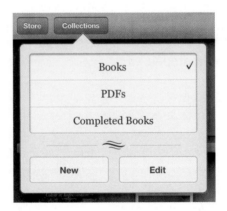

On the top-left corner of the bookshelf, tap the Collections button. In the pop-up menu that appears, you'll see two default collections: Books and PDFs. Tap New to create a new collection and enter a title in the text field. Tap Done to create your collection.

To move books into your new collection:

1. Tap the Edit button in the upper-right corner.

2. Tap the books you wish to move. Selected books contain a subtle white screen over the cover along with a blue check mark.

3. Tap Move in the upper-left corner and select the appropriate collection you'd like to move your books to from the pop-up menu.

In step 1, you'll also notice that when you tap the Edit menu a Delete button appears in the upper-left corner to delete books from your iBook library.

If you accidentally delete a book from your library:

1. Tap the Store button to enter the iBookstore.

2. Tap Purchased to display a list of purchased books.

3. As you've done with apps, tap the cloud icon next to the book's title and enter your Apple ID password to download the books a second time.

If you find it easier to look at your book titles in a list view instead of the default covers view, tap the List icon to the left of the Edit menu. Use the tabs at the bottom of the window to organize your books by title, author, category, or their position on the bookshelf.

In either the List or Bookshelf view, a search bar can be used to manually search for a specific title or author. Reveal the search bar with a short swipe down to expose the area above the top shelf or listing.

Use iBooks to Store and View PDF Files

One of the most useful, yet seldom used, features of iBooks is the ability to store and manage Portable Document File (PDF) files. I use iBooks to store PDF copies of owner's manuals, long-form articles I need to take time to read, or documents I need to refer to regularly. If you're in sales, consider storing digital copies of your catalogs, sales sheets, or promotional literature.

You can add a PDF to your iBooks library in four ways:

- Use the iTunes file transfer process described in Chapter 7.

- Use Safari to navigate to a PDF online. When the PDF document loads completely, tap the Open In iBooks button that appears near the right side of the screen, near the top of the Safari window.

- Use the Dropbox app to navigate to a PDF stored in your Dropbox folder. Tap the PDF to open it within the Dropbox viewer window, and then tap the Action icon and choose Open In | iBooks.

- E-mail the PDF to an e-mail address you can access on your iPad. Tap and hold the PDF attachment icon, and select Open In | iBooks from the pop-up menu.

View and organize your PDFs using the same techniques described previously for e-books. You can bookmark individual pages, search within PDFs, and use the Content button to view thumbnails of the PDF's pages. The Action icon in the upper-left corner of the PDF viewer allows you to e-mail or print your PDF.

iBooks vs. Other E-reader Apps for Your iPad

Like most functions of your iPad, there's more than one app for reading books on your tablet. While your choice of reader is based on your own preferences, there are some differences between e-readers that are worth mentioning.

E-reader Similarities

In terms of pure function, the top three e-readers for the iPad—iBooks, Amazon Kindle, and Barnes and Noble Nook—are quite similar. All three apps provide control over the size of text, brightness of the screen, and color themes to modify contrast for easier reading. They all also allow you to highlight, define, or make notes based on the text. All will sync between your devices so you can stop reading on your iPad and then pick up where you left off on your iPhone. At the time of this writing, the Kindle app has not yet been updated for the Retina display, making the user interface elements less sharp than the other two apps.

E-reader Differences

The largest differences among the apps stem from Apple's terms of use for in-app purchases. Apple takes a commission off all sales made through apps, making it virtually impossible for Amazon and Barnes and Noble to integrate their bookstores with their own reader apps. As a result, you need to purchase new books for these readers through their online store within the Safari app or from your computer. More of an inconvenience than a deal-breaker, this process takes you in and out of the reader app more often than occurs within iBooks.

Other, more subtle differences exist as well, like being able to share excerpts through the Kindle app, or having superior control over the appearance of your pages, like in the Nook app.

It's worth noting that books are not easily exchanged between platforms, so your purchases are effectively locked in to whichever app you decide to build your library with. Fortunately, all three apps are strong choices and all work well on your iPad.

Newsstand: Your Home for Digital Magazines and Newspapers

Newsstand is a collection point for all your subscription-based news content. It aggregates individual newspaper and magazine apps downloaded from the App Store and displays them in a bookshelf-styled drawer that slides out when you tap the Newsstand app icon on your Home screen. The Store button at the top-right corner of the Newsstand drawer delivers you to the Newsstand section within the App Store.

   The layout, navigation, and interactivity of publications is controlled by the app publishers and reflects both the unique design of the magazine or newspaper, as well as the fact that these are separate apps brought together within Newsstand for organizational purposes. Despite these differences, in the electronic issues I've read and explored, care is taken by the publishers to maintain continuity between the graphic design and layout of the printed edition and the navigational controls and conventions common to the iPad.

   One of the advantages of Newsstand is it will automatically download new issues of your subscribed periodicals and let you know when they are ready to read.

What Makes These Electronic Issues Unique?

Tablet editions of newspapers and magazines are still in their infancy. As a result, you'll find differing degrees of interactivity, usability, and additional content between periodicals. However, this technology is growing at a rapid rate, and the quality and content in digital editions is getting better every day. Today, you'll find videos replacing still photos, better links between articles, smaller file sizes for each issue, and bonus content that didn't make it in the print edition.

Publishers with periodicals that have strong visuals and that have a keen sense for design have generally adapted to this new medium quicker than other publications. The New York Times app, for example, allows you free access to the Top News section, and the clean layout makes reading a joy. Additional slideshows of still images and video clips provide a strong supplement to the written article. Photos from *National Geographic* are even more captivating on a bright, crisp display. Additional videos help you to become even more immersed in the story.

Life Outside the Newsstand

Not all magazines and newspapers are managed within the Newsstand app or found through the Newsstand Store because only periodicals that meet a specific set of criteria are eligible for inclusion in Newsstand. Apps not integrated with Newsstand exist as independent apps and will be downloaded through the App Store and displayed on your Home screen. Zinio, the oldest and largest digital newsstand, is a popular alternative. The free Zinio app provides a portal to hundreds of magazines available for single-issue purchase or annual subscription.

The Day's News Delivered to Your iPad

The news doesn't start, or end, with magazines and newspapers, particularly on your iPad. You can find most of your favorite TV, radio, and online news sources well represented in the App Store. Rather than spend time focusing on these well-known news outlets, I'm going to highlight apps and news avenues you might not be as familiar with.

RSS Readers

To keep tabs on my favorite blogs and stay current with the large volume of new blog posts written daily, I use RSS (Really Simple Syndication) readers to aggregate new blog posts and present them in an easy-to-scan layout so I can quickly identify the headlines I'm most interested in. Most RSS readers link to your Google Reader account (www.google.com/reader), which is used to store your RSS subscriptions and synchronize which blog posts you've read and which you haven't. A trio of free RSS readers have gained popularity among iPad users: Feeddler RSS (free with ads; $4.99 without ads), Feedly (free), and Mobile RSS (Free). All three link to your Google Reader account and synchronize your read and unread articles and subscriptions with Reader. Of the three apps, I found Feeddler to be the quickest for scanning a large number of headlines and identifying the most important articles, making it my go-to app for blog reading.

Socially Curated News

If you're having a difficult time keeping up with all the news, blog posts, and important articles on the Internet, you're not alone. According to the former CEO of Google, Eric Schmidt, "Every two days we create as much information as we did from the dawn of civilization up until 2003." As a result, we're suffering from information overload. To help compensate, several new apps have popped up in recent years that cull the most popular articles from the Web and your Twitter and Facebook networks to display a personalized collection of the most relevant, and important, articles for you to read. Of those, here are two I think you'll find valuable:

- **Flipboard (free)**   My favorite socially curated news service. Flipboard arranges links, status updates, and tweets in a clean, magazine-style layout that makes it easy to digest a large amount of information and find the most relevant tidbits.

- **LinkedIn (free)**   Yes, LinkedIn has taken a page from Flipboard's popularity and designed a news service that pulls from LinkedIn users' status updates and trending articles online to assemble a short, yet informative list of the most relevant articles for you to read right now. In the months since they've launched this feature, it has quickly become one of my go-to news sources for work-related information.

10

Create Movies, Music, and More on Your iPad

In previous chapters I've introduced you to a variety of ways you can use your iPad to enjoy digital videos, movies, music, and even online photo galleries. In this chapter, I'll show you how you can use your iPad to create your own digital movies, shoot photos, draw, and even make your own musical recordings. While few artists use the iPad as a stand-alone creative tool, the iPad is ideal for capturing seeds of a thought, helping you refine them, and then delivering your creation to more fully featured tools on your desktop.

iPad Photography and Video

As if your iPad wasn't multitalented enough already, Apple managed to pack into the iPad's slender frame not one, but two digital cameras. The back camera is your primary camera for photography. This camera provides ample image resolution for posting photos to the Web, sharing via e-mail, or making prints up to five by seven inches in size. When shooting video, this camera captures full high-definition (HD) resolution (1920 × 1080) video. The front camera is primarily designed to serve as a webcam for FaceTime or Skype video calls and has a relatively modest 640 × 480 pixel resolution. The photographic capabilities of this camera are primarily limited to shooting self-portraits for fun or for social media profiles. For any serious photography, you'll want to use the front-facing camera, which benefits from more megapixels and a better lens.

Shoot Photos and Video with Your iPad's Camera

The Camera app provides quick access to your camera's controls, though as you'll see in a minute, your iPad's camera can be accessed from dozens of other apps as well. The camera controls are simple, straightforward, and uncluttered, allowing you to concentrate on the artistic aspects of your photo. Use your finger to tap the most important area of the photograph, like the eyes in a portrait, to set focus. Along the right side of the screen you'll see a camera icon, which serves as your shutter button. Press it to take a picture.

In the lower-right corner is the Camera/Video switch. Slide this from the still camera icon to the video camera to jump into video mode. The shutter button changes to a red, record button. Press it to begin recording video. A small counter in the upper-right corner indicates the duration of your video recording. Tap the record button again to stop capturing video.

Along the bottom of the screen, the Options button provides access to a slender pop-up menu to enable compositional grids over your viewfinder. The Camera icon with two arrows switches between the front and back cameras.

At the far-left side, you'll see a small thumbnail of your most recently taken photo. Tap this to open the Camera Roll and view the pictures you've taken with your iPad.

The slender design of the iPad is great for watching videos, reading books, or surfing the Web, but is lousy for taking pictures or shooting video. Stabilize your iPad by placing the lower-left corner in the palm of your left hand. Bring your pinky out from your other fingers so the weight of the iPad rests on your pinky. Press your thumb securely against the frame of the iPad, creating opposing pressure with your pinky. This unorthodox grip helps me hold the iPad securely while freeing my right hand to press the shutter. I also find it easier, when photographing in landscape mode, to hold the iPad "upside down" with the back camera on the left. Otherwise, I tend to place my right hand directly over the lens.

 You can download images directly from your dSLR or other digital camera to your iPad with the iPad Camera Connection Kit ($29). For detailed instructions on its use, visit http://support.apple.com/kb/HT4101?viewlocale=en_US&locale=en_US.

Manage Your Photo and Video Library

The Photos app stores and manages photos and videos taken with your iPad's cameras and is used to store photos from other sources that you wish to store on your iPad, like a collection of favorite family photos or a slideshow of images you took with your dSLR on a recent trip.

The Photos app gives you three different ways of looking at the photos on your iPad. These headings appear at the top of the main window within the Photos app:

- **Photos** Displays thumbnails of all your photos in chronological order based on when they were added to your iPad, not when the photo was taken.

- **Photo Stream** Images shared between your iPad and your computer using iCloud.

- **Albums** Albums are groupings of photos by place, time, or subject that you create either within the Photos app on the iPad or on your computer using an application like iPhoto or Aperture that allows you to sync albums back to an iPad. You can also transfer a folder of images from your computer to your iPad using iTunes sync. Camera Roll, an album containing photos you've shot on this iPad, appears here. Tap an album thumbnail to view the contents.

View Photos and Videos on Your iPad

Within any of the three views, tap an image thumbnail to view the image in full-screen mode. Swipe left or right to move to the previous or next image in the collection. Tap a full-screen image to bring up the photo controls, which include a thumbnail bar along the bottom of the screen. Tap one of the mini-thumbnails to quickly jump to that photo within the collection, or drag your finger along the thumbnail bar to scroll through your collection at high speed. To zoom in and view the details of an image, double-tap on the image or use the open pinch gesture. To return to the standard full-screen view, double-tap again, or use the close pinch gesture. You can also use the close pinch to close the photo and return to the list of thumbnails.

To watch a video, tap the Play button in the center of the screen. During playback, the top menu bar shows a filmstrip of your video along with a playhead indicating your current location within the video clip. To the left of the filmstrip, a Play/Pause button provides control to start and stop the video.

The controls at the top-right corner of the window provide access to additional functions:

- **Edit (Photos Only)**   Provides access to basic photo-editing controls for images from your Photo Stream or those you've captured on your iPad, like rotation, crop, red-eye removal, and auto-enhance. In the Edit Photo window, you have options to revert to your original image (discard all changes and continue editing), cancel (discard all changes and return to the full-screen image), undo (remove the last change), and save (apply changes and save an adjusted copy to the photo library). Note that when you make changes to images within the Edit Photo window, your original image is preserved and all changes are made to a copy of your photo.

- **Slideshow (Photos Only)** Allows you to play a slideshow of your images. Tap the Slideshow button to reveal the slideshow options. Here, you can choose from five transitions that will be applied in between images in the slideshow, and you have the option to add music to accompany your slideshow. Slide the Play Music switch to On, and then tap the Music heading to select a track from your music library. Tap Start Slideshow to begin playing your slideshow.

 If you have an Apple TV, you can use AirPlay to wirelessly stream your slideshows from your iPad to your Apple TV. See Chapter 12 for more details.

- **Action** Use the Action icon to reveal a pop-up menu of actions to perform with your image. For photos, these include sending the image via e-mail, instant message, or Twitter; printing the photo; or setting the photo as wallpaper. For videos, you can e-mail the video, send it directly to YouTube, or copy it for use in another app.
- **Trash** Delete a photo from your photo library or Photo Stream.

To return to the thumbnail view of your current collection or album, tap the back button in the upper-left corner or use a close pinch on screen.

Use Photo Stream to Wirelessly Send Photos to Your Computer

Photo Stream, a feature built in to iCloud, automatically uploads photos taken on your iPad to your iCloud account and then downloads them to your other devices. Conversely, when you bring photos into your Photo Stream album on other devices, those photos are copied to your iPad.

To enable Photo Stream on your iPad, go to Settings | iCloud | Photo Stream and then slide the switch to On. As indicated in the note below the Photo Stream switch, Photo Stream will only upload and download images from iCloud when connected to a Wi-Fi network.

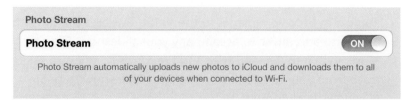

To use Photo Stream on your computer you'll need a Mac with OS X Lion 10.7.3 and iPhoto 9.2.2 or Aperture 3.2.3 or later. On Windows, you need Windows 7 or Windows Vista (Service Pack 2) and iCloud Control Panel 1.1 for Windows. The iCloud Control Panel is used to enable iCloud sync (Chapter 3) and can be downloaded at www.apple.com/icloud/setup/pc.html. On both platforms, use the iCloud Control Panel to enable Photo Stream on your computer.

When Photo Stream is enabled, on Mac, images are made available within the Photo Stream panel of either Aperture or iPhoto. On Windows, you'll be prompted to specify which folder you'd like Photo Stream images copied to on your hard drive. Once copied, Photo Stream images can be stored, edited, and published within any image-editing application.

A couple of final notes: Images are kept in your Photo Stream for 30 days. After that time, they remain on your devices, but they are no longer available for sync through iCloud unless you save them to your iPad's photo library by tapping the Action icon and selecting Save To Camera Roll. Your iPad will keep a rolling collection of your latest 1,000

Image Organization Within Photo Stream

Photo Stream organizes images by the date the image was captured, not the date the photo was added to Photo Stream. This causes the order of images to differ between the Photo and Photo Stream views and can lead to confusion.

images in the Photo Stream album. Starting with photo 1,001, images will be removed to make room for new ones. Even though older images are removed from Photo Stream on your iPad, all your Photo Stream images are preserved on your computer.

For additional information on Photo Stream, be sure to check out the Photo Stream FAQ from Apple at http://support.apple.com/kb/HT4486?viewlocale=en_US&locale=en_US.

Sort and Organize Your Photos with Albums

The Albums feature is a simple tool for grouping and organizing images in your photo library. One of the advantages of Albums is that it references the image in your image library, allowing for a single image to appear in multiple albums. As your photo library grows, albums become essential for finding the images you're looking for within an extensive photo collection.

Within the Albums tab of the Photos app, you should have at least one album, Camera Roll, created for you. Other albums may have been synchronized from your iPhoto library or were created if you downloaded photos directly from your camera to your iPad.

 I discussed your options for synchronizing photos along with other types of content from iTunes to your iPad in Chapter 3.

To create a new Album on your iPad:

1. Tap the Albums heading within the Photos app and then tap the Edit button in the top-right corner of the screen.

2. Tap the New Album button in the upper-left corner of the screen.

3. In the New Album alert, enter a name for your album.

4. Tap images from your photo library you'd like to add to your album. When selected, a blue-and-white check mark appears in the lower-right corner of the image thumbnail. Tap Done when you've selected your images.

Your new album appears within the Albums heading with your selected photos available within the new album. Tap the album thumbnail to view its contents.

To add or remove images from an album or delete an album entirely:

1. From the top level of the Albums heading, tap the Edit button in the upper-right corner of the screen.

2. To delete an album, tap the black-and-white "X" in the upper-left corner of the album thumbnail. Confirm the deletion in the Delete Album alert box. Otherwise, tap the album thumbnail to display the album's contents and view additional options.

 You cannot delete albums brought over using the iTunes file transfer outlined in the next section or the Camera Roll album.

3. To add photos to the current album, tap the Add Photos button. To remove photos from the current album, tap the photo(s) you wish to remove, and then tap the red Remove button. This removes the photo from the album, but does not delete it from your photo library.

Once you've added or removed images from your album, you'll return to the primary Albums screen.

 In step 3, you may have noticed two additional buttons: Share and Copy. The Share button allows you to select multiple images and then share them via e-mail, print, or instant message. The Copy button copies the selected photo(s) to your clipboard and makes them available for pasting in another application.

Manage Albums from iTunes   You can sync your photos and video from your computer to your iPad without having to use Apple's Aperture or iPhoto. Instead, you can specify a folder, or set of folders, on your hard drive that will be copied to your iPad. Each folder will appear as a separate album within the Photos app.

To copy a folder of images using iTunes on your computer:

1. Connect your iPad to your computer with the Universal Serial Bus (USB) cable.

2. Click your iPad's name beneath the Devices heading in the left column of iTunes and then Click the Photos heading along the top of the iPad options window.

3. Click to add a check mark to the Sync Photos From box.

4. From this pull-down menu select Choose Folder.

5. In the resulting dialog, navigate to the folder of images on your hard drive.

6. Once your folder of images is selected, choose whether you'd like to copy the folder and all subfolders contained within, or choose specific subfolders manually. Also choose whether you'd like video files copied to your iPad as well. For a list of video file formats and encoding specifications supported by the iPad, visit http://support.apple.com/kb/SP580 and scroll to the TV And Video heading.

7. Click Apply in the lower-right corner to confirm your changes and begin synchronizing your photos to your iPad.

Your photos will now appear as an album on your iPad; however, you cannot edit the contents of this album as you can with albums created on your iPad or managed through iPhoto or Aperture.

Download Photos and Videos from Your iPad to Your Computer

The Photos app is an effective tool for managing a small collection of photos or video, but if you're an avid shooter, you can quickly exceed the organizational capabilities of the Photos app and the storage capacity of your iPad. For these reasons, it is a good idea to regularly download images to your computer's hard drive for safe keeping and to more easily search for, and find, the photo you're looking for.

To download images to your hard drive, connect your iPad to your computer with your USB cable and then use the camera import feature within your favorite image-editing application (Adobe Photoshop Elements, Adobe Lightroom, etc.) to quickly download images from your iPad to your hard drive. If you don't have access to an image-editing application with this import feature, try the following:

- When you connect your iPad to your Windows-based computer, the AutoPlay dialog box should appear. Within this dialog the Import Pictures And Videos feature can assist you in copying photos and videos from your iPad to your computer.

- On the Mac, open the Image Capture application found within your Applications folder. Select your iPad within the Devices heading, choose the location you'd like your images copied to, and then click Import All.

Once you've copied photos and videos to your hard drive successfully, you can use Albums to store your very best images and delete the rest, knowing you have a copy stored on your computer.

Apps for Editing and Sharing Photos and Video

The Camera app on your iPad is a functional tool for capturing photos and videos, but it doesn't provide editing or correction tools. The Photos app has a limited set of controls for correcting photos, but it still leaves a lot to be desired. Fortunately, app developers have built a number of innovative and exciting apps to help you transform your raw footage into a finished masterpiece—using only your iPad.

Adobe's PS Express (free) provides a solid set of basic controls for improving image quality and is hard to beat for the price. Apple's iPhoto ($4.99) does a wonderful job of bringing the image adjustments and organizational tools found in the desktop version of iPhoto to the iPad. The award for my favorite photo-editing app, however, goes to Snapseed ($4.99). I was introduced to this powerful app by another professional photographer who finds he has more creative control over his images in Snapseed than he does in the professional image-editing applications on his computer.

Given the depth of the app, it does take a little time to become acquainted with all of the features, but once you do, you'll find correcting your photos to be almost as much fun as taking them. Snapseed also gives you a wide range of options for sharing your photos on social networks like Flickr, Facebook, or Twitter, and allows you to open images in Dropbox for easy transfer to your computer.

From a videographer's perspective, there are two powerhouse video-editing apps for you to choose from: Apple's iMovie ($4.99) and Avid Studio ($4.99). Of the two, iMovie is easier to learn, but Avid Studio provides more of the controls you'd expect in a video-editing application for cutting together your masterpiece. Both offer several options for exporting and sharing your video, including the ability to export to a companion application on your computer, whether iMovie (Mac only) or Avid Studio (Windows only).

Despite being a little tricky to learn, Avid Studio delivers more sophisticated video-editing tools like the razor blade for cutting or splitting a video clip and a Precision Trimmer window.

When you launch the app, Avid Studio scans your iPad and builds a media library for you to draw clips from. These photos, videos, audio tracks, and music are all neatly arranged within corresponding tabs on the left side of the window. When working on a new project, most users will want to begin dragging clips into the Storyboard, a tool for quickly building your project and arranging the sequence of clips used to tell your story. More experienced editors will probably want to first trim media using the pretrimming tool before adding clips to the Storyboard. In the lower quarter of the screen are the project timeline tracks: one video and three separate audio tracks for adding music, voiceover, or sound effects. Once your edit is completed, heighten the production value with transitions to seamlessly move between clips and then export a video file (up to 720 p), e-mail your video, or upload directly to Facebook or YouTube. If you work with the Avid Studio desktop application on your Windows computer, you can export your project file and continue to refine your movie on your computer.

Drawing, Writing, and Illustration

Although my drawing skills are limited to crude outlines and stick figures, that doesn't stop me from having a blast experimenting with the brilliant drawing apps that are designed for the iPad. Of course, the ability to draw can be serious business as well. The ability to sketch out a diagram in a business meeting or take a picture of a room and then draw in the new location of walls and light fixtures for a remodeling project helps to easily communicate abstract concepts.

Apps for Drawing and Sketching

In my experiments with a half-dozen drawing apps on the iPad, two quickly became my favorites: Paper by 53 (free) and Autodesk's Sketchbook Pro ($4.99). These two rose to the top, in large part, because of the quality of the brushes they offer. Sketchbook Pro comes with a wide selection of brushes, from fine-lined markers to soft air-brushes, to apply lines and color exactly where you want them. Paper by 53 comes with a basic fountain pen for line drawing and offers additional brushes through in-app purchases.

Sketchbook Pro provides the ability to import photos from your photo library and the creation of additional layers to fine-tune your artwork. Paper by 53 eschews these features in favor of an aesthetic not unlike an artist's notebook, where the primary function of the app is to sketch ideas or moments and let nothing else get in the way.

Use a Stylus for Better Drawing and Handwriting

Your finger is a pretty crude instrument for drawing or writing. Several manufacturers create iPad-safe styluses to make working on the iPad a lot more like drawing and writing on paper. I particularly like the feel of the Bamboo Stylus Solo ($30) from Wacom. The barrel of the stylus has a nice heft to it, and the nib (the drawing tip) provides a wonderfully responsive feel against the glass of the Multi-Touch screen.

Both my drawing skill and writing legibility improve dramatically when using a stylus over the tip of my finger.

Handwriting for the iPad

A variety of iPad apps allow you to draw or write notes using your finger or a stylus in lieu of a pen or pencil. The most popular of these apps, Penultimate ($0.99), is designed like a paper notebook and is ideal for taking notes at meetings or conferences, sketching out a floor plan, or writing up a "back of the napkin" business plan. One of the advantages of Penultimate is that it allows you to connect your Penultimate notebook with other web applications like Evernote or Dropbox. When you send your handwritten Penultimate notes to Evernote, the handwriting-recognition module within Evernote will convert your written notes into text that can be searched from within your Evernote database.

Music Creation and Editing

What if you could strum your iPad like a guitar, tap out the notes of a piano melody, or use it as a turntable for your next party? The Multi-Touch screen of the iPad is a terrific control surface for all musicians, from hacks like me tinkering with music-making to serious professionals layering together multi-instrument tracks. The Multi-Touch screen allows developers to build apps that allow musicians to think about and interact with music in innovative ways.

Apps for Amateur Musicians

Even if you don't know a G chord from a C chord, you can still enjoy the music-making process on the iPad. I've pulled together a short collection of apps for anyone to get started. Keep in mind, music apps aren't just for adults—they are great tools to get children excited about music and begin learning the fundamentals.

GarageBand   When it comes to music-making apps, GarageBand ($4.99) rules the roost for its ability to bring a sophisticated level of music-making prowess to a tablet application that's easy enough for nonmusicians to have a blast with.

Within GarageBand, you have a comprehensive collection of instruments to choose from. Some, like the drum kit, keyboard, audio recorder, and guitar amp, are tablet versions of their analog counterparts and the sophistication of the music you can make with these instruments is determined by your musical training and ability to keep tempo. Bundled alongside are "smart instruments" that nonmusicians can experiment with and make music in an intuitive way. For example, I once tried to scratch out a simple tune on a violin and the result sounded like cat's claws on a chalkboard. Within GarageBand, however, I can dial up the Smart Strings instruments and take command of an orchestra. Taps produce pizzicato notes, while dragging my finger mimics the bowing of the string section. Although real musicians might consider this cheating, I enjoy it because it's fun and provides a basic introduction to musical theory through the use of scales.

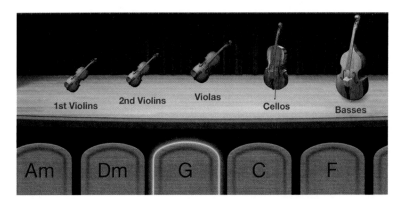

Within the GarageBand app, you can record your sessions and then edit, loop, cut, and mix tracks before exporting them to YouTube, SoundCloud, Facebook, iTunes, or e-mail. You can also transfer the original project files through iTunes on your computer to open your GarageBand projects on your Mac using the GarageBand application. If you're into collaborative music-making, up to four musicians can connect their iPads using Wi-Fi or Bluetooth to make and record music collaboratively. For these reasons, and many more, I highly recommend

GarageBand as the starting point for exploring the iPad's potential for music-making.

Loopseque   Loopseque (Lite, free; Full $5.99) is a beat-making app to help you build electronic beats for music beds or to serve as the starting point for a more complex song. Loopseque is unique in the way the beats are arranged on a circular grid, which visually underscores the circular nature of repetitive rhythms. With Loopseque you can build off a number of preset beats, create your own from scratch, or enter Master Class mode and learn how professionals build catchy beats. The free version has a lot of functionality to explore and experiment with, but you'll have to purchase the full version to have the ability to copy or save your tracks for use outside Loopseque.

Tabletop   A modular audio environment for your iPad, Tabletop (free) is on the verge of being too advanced for my skill level, but I wanted to include it here because of the wide range of options included in the free version and the amount of fun I've had just tinkering with the mixers, turntables, keyboards, touchpads, and sequencers. Several preset tracks serve as starting points, and there are a number of excellent tutorials online to help you set up your own Tabletop to really make it sing. And by sing, I mean you can create catchy electronic songs, hooks, and beats and then save them in the .wav format for use in desktop audio-editing applications, copy them to use in other apps, or export a finished track to SoundCloud. Intermediate and advanced musicians will enjoy using a broader range of instruments, which can be purchased directly from within the app.

Apps for Musicians

I sat down with professional musician and music producer Steve Heap (www.VuetoneStudios.com) to get his recommendations on apps for experienced music creators.

Djay   The Djay app ($4.99) is a blast for beginners as well as experienced DJs. Use the two turntables to DJ your next party by mixing and scratching songs from your iTunes library. Experienced DJs appreciate the beats per minute (BPM) sync and loop features for more sophisticated transitions. Djay also integrates well with other iPad-based editors, like GarageBand, and can save high-resolution audio files for further editing on your laptop.

DM1 Drum Machine   When I create music, it usually begins with a drumbeat, and Drum Machine ($4.99) has become my sketchpad for trying out new ideas. What's great about this app is that it gives me professional-grade controls over the type of drum kit used, the mix between instruments, and effects applied to each track. Once I have a track I like, I can export it to iTunes, prep it for e-mail, or use audiocopy to bring it into another application to combine it with other elements.

Beat Maker 2   In my opinion, Beat Maker 2 ($19.99) is the best beat-making and advanced music-making app. The number of instruments you have to choose from and the editing and postprocessing capabilities are immense. This app turns your iPad into a mobile music-making powerhouse.

In addition to Steve's excellent recommendations, you may want to check out the iOS Music and You blog (http://iosmusicandyou.com/) run by Chip Boaz. He has a number of excellent app reviews along with tutorials to get you started with several professional music-making apps. Now go make some music!

11

The iPad for Every Day of Your Life

By now, you have an idea of how the iPad can keep you organized and informed. The great thing is that it can do so much more than that. It can be your personal assistant, your assistant chef, teacher ... and the list goes on. Since the uses for the iPad are virtually boundless and cannot be encompassed in one book, my goal for this chapter is to show you how a collection of apps makes the iPad an invaluable tool for a broad spectrum of activities. Think of the apps I recommend as a "starter kit" to help you begin your exploration into the deeper world of apps. Explore and enjoy!

Business and Productivity

For many people, the work/life balance has settled into an equilibrium of being always on, always connected, and ready to respond to work requests 24 hours a day, seven days a week. The portable iPad offers you a suite of versatile tools for managing your work, your clients, and your career to hopefully get your work done quickly and help you carve out a little time for relaxation.

Word Processing and Spreadsheets

Next to e-mail, business users must be able to read, edit, and share Microsoft Word documents and Excel spreadsheets. Although there is no official Microsoft Office for the iPad, a number of apps allow you to work with Microsoft Office documents, and other word-processing apps can export documents in file formats that Microsoft Word is able to read.

The most popular of these Microsoft Office analogues is Quickoffice Pro HD ($19.99), a robust app with the sole purpose of working with Microsoft Word docs, Excel spreadsheets, and PowerPoint presentations. Quickoffice Pro HD is a great choice for users of Windows computers because it strongly mimics the design aesthetic of Microsoft Office applications and will be a familiar companion to the trio of computer applications. The app does break with several of Apple's design and navigation conventions, which several users have commented detracts from the usability of the app.

If you're accustomed to working on a Mac computer, you'll probably find Apple's iWork apps, Pages and Numbers ($9.99 each), to be more familiar than Quickoffice Pro HD. As you'd expect from an Apple-designed app, Pages and Numbers share a clean, elegant design aesthetic and are more closely integrated to the navigation and design conventions you've become accustomed to on the iPad. My biggest complaint with Pages and Numbers is the lack of integration with other file-transfer and file-sharing services like Dropbox and Evernote. I find the file transfer through iTunes to be a clunky process, which makes e-mail the primary means of delivering iWork documents to my computers. I do appreciate that I'm able to e-mail my iWork documents in their native file formats, their Microsoft Office equivalents (.doc, .xls), or as a Portable Document File (PDF) file, which helps me deliver a file compatible with whichever set of applications my recipient is using.

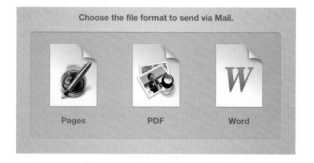

If you and your colleagues have moved to the cloud-based Google Docs for document sharing, you can access your Google Docs through the Safari browser app or the Google app (free), a versatile tool for managing your Google web applications. The primary downside to using Google Docs is the lack of offline access. While this is less of a problem for Wi-Fi + Cellular users, who can be connected wherever they go, the Google app won't be usable on an airplane unless you have in-flight Wi-Fi, which often costs extra.

If integration with Microsoft Office is less important than having a clean, easy-to-use word processor, you might take a look at Daedalus Touch ($4.99). An elegant, minimalist app for writing, Daedalus Touch feels like what a native iPad word processor should be, with gesture controls for navigating between documents. Daedalus Touch is designed with an emphasis on writing, which is clear from the thoughtful design of the document and keyboard features. For example, to make typing easier on the iPad, they've added a collection of commonly used keys along the top of the keyboard to prevent you from having to interrupt your writing to dive into the second or third keyboard to find a colon or em dash. Daedalus Touch allows you to export your documents via e-mail and .txt, .pdf, and .epub formats, as well as copying text to the clipboard or printing via AirPrint.

Presentations

For business road warriors who often fly across the country to deliver a short presentation, the thought of ditching a laptop in favor of an iPad is certainly tantalizing. SlideShark (free), an app for managing and presenting PowerPoint documents, is a great solution. After you create an account in SlideShark, you upload your PowerPoint document to their online service and then can download it to your iPad for delivering your presentation. In my experience, the service works smoothly and preserves the design and transitions of your original presentation with a high degree of fidelity. Unfortunately, with SlideShark, you are unable to make changes to the content of your PowerPoint slides, so if you notice a typo, you need to make the change to the original document, reupload it, and then download it again on your iPad.

Quickoffice HD Pro, discussed earlier, allows you to create and edit PowerPoint documents, and may be a better option if you frequently need to modify graphics, update text or graphics, or change the intro slides of your presentations.

For Mac users, the Keynote app ($9.99) is an effective companion to the Keynote presentation application on your computer and can be used to deliver native Keynote (.key) files along with PowerPoint presentations. The tools to create and edit a Keynote presentation are effective, but can be slow when compared to performing the same tasks on your computer. I recommend building your Keynote presentation on your computer and then transferring it to your iPad via iTunes or Dropbox. From there, use the Keynote app to make refinements to the presentation and deliver it to your audiences. For the best results, you'll want to spend some time during the design and planning stage of your presentation to ensure your Keynote is iPad-compatible. For example, the font selection on your iPad is limited when compared to your computer. You can use the versatile workhorse Gill Sans on your computer and the iPad, but the Stone Sans ITC you use for your company identity isn't supported on the iPad and will be changed to an alternate font. By itself, the font substitution isn't that big of a deal, however, the differences between the size and character attributes of the two fonts can cause big problems for your layout. Most of the common transitions are retained, and graphics like illustrations, photos, and videos should transfer accurately to your iPad, though I recommend testing your presentation thoroughly before you jump into an important presentation.

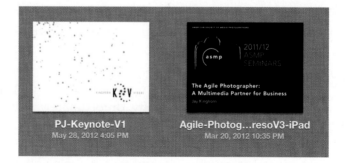

For a list of fonts supported by Keynote for the iPad, visit http://support.apple.com/kb/HT4637.

To connect your iPad to a standard Video Graphics Array (VGA) projector cable, you'll need the Apple VGA adapter cable ($29). If you're connecting to a liquid crystal display (LCD) television with a High Definition Multimedia Interface (HDMI) cable, you'll want the Apple Digital AV Adapter ($39).

VPN and Remote Login

If you work for a larger company, you may be able to connect to your work e-mail and access files on your company's servers using the iPad's built-in VPN (virtual private network) support. VPN provides additional security for connecting to shared networks like a company intranet or private servers. For this reason, many larger companies have their employees connect to their work files using VPN exclusively.

To set up VPN on your iPad, you'll need to talk to your company's IT department to receive information on the type of VPN connection supported by your company's network along with the required login information.

Business Utilities

The business uses of the iPad aren't limited to performing traditional computing tasks. In fact, these nontraditional uses of the iPad make it a powerhouse of a business tool. In this section, I'll address some specific business scenarios where the iPad really excels.

In-Person Meetings

Despite the range of online tools for conducting business, there's still no substitute for sitting down with a client face to face. In these meetings, an iPad is far friendlier to have on the table than a laptop; it doesn't obscure eye contact between the participants and is easy to pass back and forth to display sales sheets and order forms, or preview a webpage. An iPad is also much quicker to power up to access a single document than a laptop, making it a great tool to share your business literature, promotional material, or a multimedia portfolio of your work.

Prior to your meeting, load your iPad with portfolio images, testimonial videos, or PDF copies of your literature. A shared Dropbox folder can be valuable for ensuring all staff has access to current sales documents and literature. PDFs can be brought into iBooks for easy viewing, and an album of photos and videos stored in the Photos app is perfect for showing your past work to future clients.

Consider using a drawing app like Paper, SketchBook Pro, or Penultimate to draw quick schematics, illustrate a point, or use as a negotiating tool. Write the price, quantity, and other key negotiating points on the screen and leave it on the table where everyone can see. As negotiations change, add or subtract items or change prices so everyone at the table has the same basis of information to work from.

Conferences, Lectures, and Meetings

When you aren't the one doing the talking, the iPad's ability to take notes and organize your thoughts on the material being presented makes it a valuable tool for conferences, lectures, and business meetings. Use the Notes app as a simple note-taking tool and sync notes to your computer using iCloud, or use one of several handwriting apps like Penultimate ($0.99), Ghostwriter Notes ($4.99), or a hybrid typing/writing app like SoundNote ($4.99) (Figure 11-1). As discussed in Chapter 10, I'm a big advocate of using a stylus to make writing on the iPad much easier. Also look for apps with a "wrist guard" feature that allows you to rest your wrist on the iPad's screen without affecting the Multi-Touch screen.

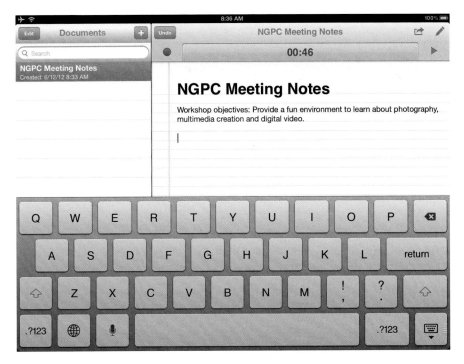

Figure 11-1 *SoundNote allows you to record audio of a lecture or meeting while taking notes.*

 If you're using an app with a wrist-guard feature, you might need to disable the four-finger multitasking gestures, as the iPad can sometimes mistake your wrist for a cluster of fingers. Disable this feature by choosing Settings | General | Multitasking Gestures.

Point-of-Sale Terminal

On a recent trip to San Francisco, a majority of the small businesses I visited had replaced their traditional point-of-sale terminal with an iPad. The most popular apps that help you accept payment by way of your iPad are Square (free), a credit card processing app, and Register (free), Square's sister software for using your iPad as a point-of-sale terminal.

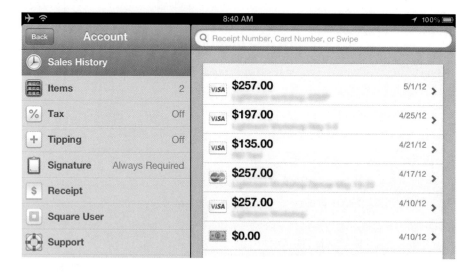

The iPad as Your Social Media Hub

The rapid growth of social media services like Facebook, Twitter, and Pinterest has firmly solidified the era of instant communication. Through a range of devices and online services we have more options to keep in touch with our friends, family, and social networks. If you think of each of these services as spokes on a wheel, the iPad serves as the hub, a central location for accessing all your social networks and making video calls over the Internet.

Send Text Messages from Your iPad

The Messages app allows you to send SMS (Short Message Service) or MMS (Multimedia Messaging Service) over Wi-Fi or cellular networks to users of other iOS 5 devices. One of the unique aspects of Messages compared to other text-messaging apps on the iPad is that your messages are delivered to all devices logged into your Apple ID.

This way, when I receive a text message, I can read and respond to it on my iPhone or my iPad, whichever is more convenient for me.

The first time you launch the Messages app, you'll be prompted to enter your Apple ID. When you've entered your account information, tap Sign In. In the next window, confirm your Apple ID as the primary e-mail address you'd like to use for receiving messages.

When you've signed in successfully, you'll see the Messages window. On the left column will be the people you've communicated with using Messages and on the right is a window for composing and reading your messages.

To create a new message:

1. In the To field, type the name, phone number, or e-mail address of the person you'd like to send a message to. Messages will check the phone number against your contacts list and auto-fill the correct phone number or e-mail address if your recipient is listed in your contacts database. Remember, you can only use Messages to send text messages to users of iOS 5 devices. As you type your recipient information, a blue chat icon to the right of the recipient's phone number indicates their account is recognized by Messages and can receive your text message.

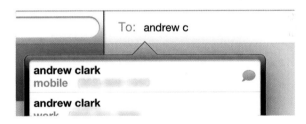

   If you enter recipient information and their name turns red, this indicates they are not using an iOS 5 device and cannot receive text messages using the Messages app.

2. In the text field immediately above the keyboard, type your message. Alternatively, if you'd prefer to send a multimedia message, tap the camera icon to the left of the text field and choose between Take Photo Or Video and Choose Existing.

If you choose to select an existing photo or video, tap the Camera Roll or Photo Stream heading to select your media. If you're sending a video, the Choose Video pop-up menu allows you to scroll through the video and trim the length by sliding the ends of the video thumbnail window toward the center.

When satisfied, tap Use and your photo or video will be attached to your message.

3. Tap Send to deliver your message.

Messages is easy to use and is tightly integrated into your iPad's operating system. Unfortunately, it only allows you to send and receive messages between Apple devices with iOS 5 installed, which omits a lot of the world. Fortunately, there are text-messaging alternatives to Messages for your iPad.

TextMe (free) is a versatile text-messaging application that allows you to send and receive SMS and MMS text messages. When you sign up for your free TextMe account, you receive a phone number that is used for delivering text messages and can be used (with the companion iPhone app) for making phone calls and retrieving voice messages.

Connect to Your Social Networks

With your iPad you'll never be far from your social networks. Most of the major social networks—Facebook, Twitter, and LinkedIn—have iPad apps, while a few holdouts like MySpace, Google +, Pinterest, and Tumblr only offer iPhone apps at this time. Even if your favorite social network doesn't offer an iPad app, you can still access the site through Safari just as you would on your computer.

Send and Receive Messages from Twitter

Twitter, as you probably well know, is a micro-blogging service that's gained a worldwide user base in only a few short years. The premise of Twitter is simple: Write a 140-character message, click Send, and it's made available to anyone who "follows" you, Twitter parlance for indicating they've added you to their Twitter network.

To get started, open the Settings app and tap the Twitter heading. This brings up your Twitter preferences. If you haven't already installed the Twitter app, a button at the top of Twitter's preferences allows you to do just that. Below are two fields to enter your Twitter user name and password. If you don't already have an account, tap the Create New Account button at the bottom.

When you're signed in, you're given the option to add a second account in the Add Account heading. Immediately below this heading you'll find the Update Contacts button. This searches your contacts database and adds Twitter user names, called handles, to the people in your database who use Twitter. When completed, the number of updated contacts is displayed below the Update Contacts button.

The final heading in Preferences, Allow, gives you the opportunity to link your Twitter account with other apps on your iPad. This useful feature makes apps like Showyou or Flipboard more powerful, because they aggregate the news that's shared on your Twitter network. Use the switches to enable or disable an app's access to your Twitter account.

Send Tweets from the Twitter App

While the options within Safari are limited to tweeting a simple web link with a message, the Twitter app offers a boatload of options for reading tweets from the people you follow; tracking direct messages or mentions; managing your lists; or searching for a person, topic, or hashtag. If these terms are foreign to you, check out Jessica Hiche's simple, and humorous, introduction to Twitter titled "Mom, This Is How Twitter Works": www.jhische.com/twitter/.

To send tweets from the Twitter app, tap the Compose button in the lower-left corner, type your tweet, and tap Send. This window also gives you a few options:

@	You can address your tweet to a specific person, for example, @jaykinghorn: your iPad book is really useful! This message is visible to the world, but would appear in my Mentions feed. When I write back @yourTwitterName: Thanks for the great note! It will appear in your Mentions feed.
#	The hashtag is a way of associating your tweet with a given topic like #superbowl or #academyawards. Twitter users subscribe to feeds from a given hashtag.
◉	The camera icon allows you to add a photo or video stored on your iPad or take a new photo to enliven your tweet.
◢	This icon adds geographic information to your tweet.
⚙	Located at the bottom of the page, this provides quick access to your Twitter settings, including advanced options for specifying which web services you'd like to use for posting photos or video and reading posts later.

There's a lot to using Twitter and, unfortunately, there simply isn't the space to provide a comprehensive tutorial on how you can use it to connect with friends, influence discussions, or promote your business. Fortunately, there are lots of great resources online.

 When you're in Safari and find a webpage, killer photo, or video you'd like to share with your Twitter followers, tap the Action icon to the left of the URL bar, and then tap Tweet. The Tweet window appears along with a thumbnail of the article you're sharing with your followers. Tap Send to deliver your tweet.

There are also loads of apps for managing your Twitter accounts for business or personal use. The ones I use most are TweetDeck (free) and Flipboard (free). Other popular apps to consider are HootSuite (free with HootSuite subscription) for business, Tweetbot ($2.99), or Twitterific (Free).

Configure Social Network Notifications

One of the advantages of installing an app from your social networking sites instead of solely using Safari is the ability to receive notifications on comments, followers, and posts through the Notification Center or through iPad alerts. In Chapter 2, I provided instructions on configuring alerts and specifying which apps are displayed in the Notification Center. You may wish to re-read that section to brush up on iPad alerts and notifications, or jump directly to Settings | Notifications to configure which apps are included in your Notification Center.

Make Video and Voice Calls with Skype

In Chapter 6 I introduced you to FaceTime, Apple's video-calling application. While it's great to be able to call other iPad, iPhone, and Mac users, it can be limiting when you want to call someone who isn't part of the Apple tribe. I tend to use Skype extensively when traveling internationally to keep in touch with my family without spending a small fortune for international phone calls. The Skype app (free) allows you to conduct free video calls with other Skype users or make voice calls to any landline or mobile phone. Rates for these calls vary from just over 2 cents per minute for international calls to landlines in select countries, to just over 30 cents per minute for calls to mobile phones in less populous countries like Albania or Nigeria. Skype works with Wi-Fi and cellular data connections and, in my experience, does a great job of adapting video streaming on less-than-optimal Internet connections. Skype has become our favorite app to keep in touch while traveling and to connect with my family spread across thousands of miles.

Children and Young Adults

In this book, I've highlighted many ways the iPad is changing the way adults interact with information. I'd be amiss to not include how the iPad is revolutionizing how children and young adults play and learn. Far more than a modernized "electronic babysitter," an iPad can be a portable learning center, with the Multi-Touch screen being much easier for younger children to use than a computer mouse and keyboard. As with any technology, it is up to parents to decide when, where, and for how long the iPad should be used by their children. To help you decide what's most appropriate for your child, I've included some of my favorite apps for children of all ages based on recommendations from the nonprofit group Common Sense Media (www.commonsensemedia.org/) on what to look for in selecting apps for your children.

Are iPads Harmful to Young Children?

An ongoing survey of more than 2,000 parents conducted by CNET is finding that a whopping 95 percent of them allow their toddlers to use the iPad and other touch screen devices. It's no wonder kids love touch screen devices so much; they are stimulating, colorful, accessible, and easy to handle. While it takes years to determine the effects of new technologies on small children, and the iPad is just two years old, studies on the immediate benefits of iPad use for kids are promising. They suggest that interactive technology, like iPads, iPhones, and Androids, when paired with appropriate apps, can help kids learn.

A recent study by the Michael Cohen Group, as part of the U.S. Department of Education's Ready to Learn program, found that for children ages 2 through 8, several types of learning occur during interaction with apps on the iPad. According to the study, "Young Children, Apps & iPad," children learn from the iPad how to use a game and its rules, the tasks associated with completing the game (like matching or counting), and the use of skills that can be applied to other types of games and play. In addition, "engaging with creative app activities often shifts the child's focus away from the subjective experience of winning or losing to a personal-best competition," which can be quite rewarding.

Protect Your iPad from Kid Chaos

The iPad can be a very fun educational tool for little hands and minds. However, those sticky fingerprints and tendency to handle things with less care than an adult can do a number on the iPad.

First, I recommend getting a good cover for the iPad to protect the screen and make the iPad a bit more bump-proof. Big Grips (biggrips.com) offers lightweight, durable, easy-to-clean, large, squishy frames in a variety of colors that make the iPad fun for little hands to grip and manipulate. It also comes with a stand to allow the iPad to become a mini-TV. There are much more robust covers on the market, but this one seems to be a good, colorful option with a reasonable price tag of about $35.

You may be able to help your iPad be easier to handle for kids, but you'll be hard-pressed to keep it from getting tons of fingerprints. To clean the iPad screen, gently wipe it down using a soft, slightly damp, lint-free cloth.

You are now armed with the tools to help your child enjoy the iPad. Be warned, you may end up having to buy a new one for yourself since it will be difficult to reclaim once it becomes their favorite plaything.

Types of iPad Apps for Children

I've seen firsthand how the iPad, when coupled with useful, appropriate apps, can delight my toddler. I'm convinced, with limitations on how much time kids spend with the device, it can be a great learning tool. I've outlined three types of apps kids find engaging and educational:

- **Digital book apps** Perhaps the most engaging and educational of all kid-centered fun, digital books bring kids into the story and sometimes, even make them the main character. This new way of telling stories offers kids the option to not only read words on a screen, but to immerse themselves in the story through interactive games and tasks and engaging video and other audio.

- **Creativity apps** Creativity apps are especially attractive to kids because they are able to freely build, create, and draw, with the option to start over if their creation is not to their liking. Creativity apps' use of color, blended with open-ended, artistic results, speaks to kids' individual strengths and interests. For instance, one child may use a storytelling app to draw elaborate characters for their story, while another child may spend the majority of their time with the app writing the storyline.

- **Gaming apps** Well-designed games, with clearly defined sequential levels and autonomy for the child in their gaming experience, can challenge and educate children. Multiplayer options (if you choose to allow this) can help teach children about the challenges of winning and losing and about teamwork.

Recommended Apps for All Kids

The third-generation iPad and its Retina display make for a glorious visual experience for kids and adults of all ages. This lovely screen lends itself well to the color and action of many apps for kids. But all apps are not created equal. I've found that big color and lots of movement can just mask a poorly made app. On the flipside, there is a plethora of engaging apps that teach your child while they think they're just having fun. Many of these apps are also great for use in tandem, so you and your child can learn together. Note: I've listed app ratings for each recommended app in this section. Descriptions of the app ratings can be found in Chapter 7.

Apps for Toddlers (0–4)

According to the Cohen Group, very young children naturally learn through concrete, tactile experiences, and then progress to more conceptual and abstract understanding. In this way, the iPad is a great complement to young children's natural learning processes, since it offers first the interactive experiences and then options for deeper learning and problem solving.

Millie Was Here: Meet Millie (free, 4+ rating, subsequent games and stories, $0.99–$3.99 each) A multiple award-winning interactive book, *Millie Was Here* is a story about a very special dog and her unique talents. The app effectively uses touch and sound features, making for an engrossing and enchanting experience. Your child, and you, will love Millie.

Goodnight Safari (free, 4+) Gorgeous drawings, interactivity, and optimization for the third-generation iPad's Retina display make this book a little gem for children ages two to four. Kids can choose to have the book narrated or read it on their own. Throughout the story, readers are prompted to perform tasks on the touch screen, like helping a zebra find its mom and lulling a monkey to sleep. This is a great app for bedtime.

Jib Jab Junior Books (free, 4+, subsequent books, $3.99/month or $7.99/story)   From the popular Jib Jab site that knows personalization best comes this book series that makes your child the star of the show. Cute, engaging stories use a photo of your child's face (or your face for that matter) to complete the main character. The app is free, and so is a monthly book, but individual books are an added cost.

Apps for Young Kids (5–9)

For young children between the ages of five and nine, socialization and creativity are key, and there are apps to support this unique stage of development. The child advocacy nonprofit Common Sense Media suggests that when choosing apps for this age group, "go beyond the usual arcade games" to apps that give kids the opportunity to express themselves creatively through coloring or express their emotions.

Intro to Geography - North America ($1.99, 4+)

I'm going to admit that a short while ago I did not know the shape or exact location of Nicaragua. But after checking out Intro to Geo, from Montessorium, I now can identify the country's shape and flag and locate it on a map, nor will I ever forget. This is testament to this effective and fun learning app that, based on the proven methodology of Montessori, teaches children about North America through an engaging and methodical process.

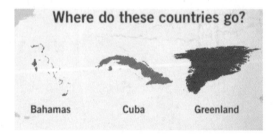

Story Patch ($2.99, 4+)   Though this app could be fun for toddlers with a parent's assistance, it was specifically designed with early readers in mind because it allows them to be creative without forcing them to create illustrations from scratch. Young kids can choose whether to write their own story or have the app write a story for them. Either way, it then instructs them on how to use more than 800 illustrations to create their own personalized book. The Search feature makes it easy to find just the right illustrations. Note: After kids enter a search term in the Search window, make sure they hit RETURN on the iPad keyboard to get results. Of course, kids love to share their work, so they have the option to send their masterpiece in PDF format via e-mail to Mom, Dad, and friends.

My Story ($1.99, 4+ rating)   I find this app to be a reasonably priced, fun-to-use, creative powerhouse. Children create their own storybook by adding blank pages to illustrate, write, or make an audio recording of their story. The drawing and page creation options are plentiful enough without being overwhelming and offer kids free rein to draw anything their heart desires. Particularly nice is the ability to add photos to the book from the iPad's camera or photo library. You can share the stories with anyone who has an iPhone or iPad via e-mail and update the story to iBook with a fairly easy transition. However, e-mailing the story to a computer is clunky, and the design of the book is not always well preserved.

Apps for Tweens (9–11) and Teens (12+)

If you haven't already spoken with your child about appropriate online behavior, it's probably time, as they are most likely interacting with other children online in games and on social networks. Common Sense Media suggests that parents and guardians start setting time limits for the iPad and be on the lookout for multiplayer capabilities in apps, and the ability to restrict this feature if you'd prefer. See Chapter 2 for a refresher on enabling and setting restrictions.

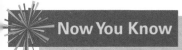

Now You Know   Where'd My Apps Go?

Once you set restrictions on apps, be aware that some of your apps may disappear from view on your iPad. For instance, if you own the Frankenstein app (which has a 12+ rating), you will no longer be able to see the app on your iPad if you restrict 12+ apps. Movie and TV show ratings you've restricted will be visible in the Videos app, but cannot be purchased. To be able to purchase and view apps, movies, and TV shows that you've restricted, you'll need to change your restrictions during adult use and purchasing and then add your child restrictions back in once you are finished using your iPad.

The Fantastic Flying Books of Mr. Morris Lessmore ($4.99, 4+)   The short film included in this app won the 2012 Academy Award for Best Animated Short Film. That fact alone should provide a clue that this is no ordinary interactive book. The Fantastic Flying Books app tells the story of Morris Lessmore, whose life is thrown into disarray by a terrible storm. He finds that when he loses his words and his stories in the storm, the color disappears from his life. Fortunately, some magical friends help him reclaim his words and write his story for the rest of his life. Younger children will enjoy the book, but older kids will find more meaning and be better able to discuss with adults the messages the story contains.

Strip Designer ($2.99, 9+)   Kids become their own comic designer through this clever app that allows them to build a story based on photos from their own life or their own drawings. The tools are sophisticated without being difficult and offer numerous creative options. Completed comic strips can be exported in a number of versatile file formats or posted to social networks. If you have multiple Apple devices, your comic strips can be saved to the cloud, making them accessible on other devices for further editing.

GarageBand ($4.99, 4+)   Allow your tween or teen to explore the world of music on the iPad. GarageBand's smart instruments make it easy to get started and, as their skill level grows, this app will grow with them and can be used as a recording device for real instruments like guitars and keyboards. Check out Chapter 10 for more music app recommendations.

Frankenstein for iPad and iPhone ($4.99, 12+)   An adaptation of Mary Shelly's novel *Frankenstein,* this book provides a different take on the classic novel by offering readers choices throughout the book— each choice leading them on a different story path. The app is richly designed, and the writing is crisp and engaging. The app provides access to both the original *Frankenstein* and this creative adaptation by Dave Morris to offer more mature teens a fun, engrossing reading experience.

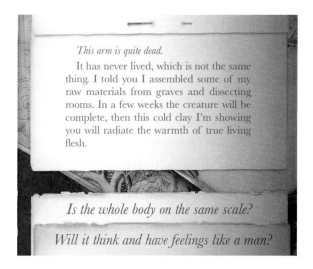

Tweens and teens will also find the educational resources outlined in the following section to be entertaining learning tools to accompany their school work. As companions to their formal education, apps can help drive home lessons taught in the classroom.

Learning, Education, and Reference

Learning and education represent perhaps the greatest opportunities for the iPad to radically reshape our lives. For hundreds of years, our learning has been derived from books and lectures. Today, educators like Sir Ken Robinson feel this methodology, coupled with an emphasis on rote learning, is inadequate for today's world. The iPad serves as a learning tool that could transform education for our, and future, generations.

What makes the iPad such a powerful tool for education is the interactivity and exploration that it brings to a topic. When curricula are designed for this medium, the emphasis shifts to an interactive, nonlinear learning style that engages multiple modes of learning (reading, listening, participating) and allows for greater synthesis between ideas than traditional learning methods.

Expand Your Knowledge at iTunes U

Begin your explorations with the iTunes U app (free). Here, you'll find a library of hundreds of courses from top-notch universities and learning institutions covering topics from general education, for example, general chemistry, to highly specialized instruction like the courses on immunology from the Albert Einstein College of Medicine. The layout of the iTunes U store isn't as well organized and as easy to use as the iBookstore or App Store; however, the course materials available for free are excellent and deserve a thorough exploration.

Once subscribed, you'll find your courses organized on your iTunes U bookshelf. The commands and structure of your iTunes U bookshelf mirrors your iBooks bookshelf. For instructions on how to reorganize, remove, or arrange courses on your iTunes U bookshelf, see Chapter 9.

Interactive Tools for Learning

A collection of iPad apps provides insight and new perspectives to common topics like art, anatomy, astronomy, chemistry, and geography. Their interactivity allows users to make connections with material that would otherwise be difficult to accomplish in a traditional textbook. Art.com's Art Circles (free) places a collection of works of art on four separate wheels. These four circles provide new ways of associating works of art.

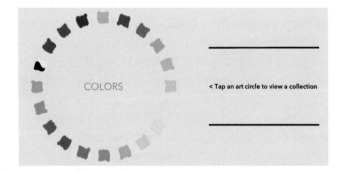

COLORS

< Tap an art circle to view a collection

Several beautiful apps help you make sense of the stars you see in the night sky, but few can beat GoSkyWatch for its ease of use, rich graphics, and attractive price tag (free). GoSkyWatch uses your location and the orientation of the iPad to organize the display of constellations in the night sky to match your field of view. Informational overlays show more information on the constellation, including the scientific names and when the constellation will be visible in your sky. To change your orientation from the celestial to the terrestrial, consider Google Earth (free) as a multipurpose tool for trip planning and researching hikes, but also as a valuable tool for learning geography. There is something magical about the ability to pilot a virtual camera to any point on the earth and fly over the terrain. It lends a deeper appreciation to geography than does a simply illustrated map.

Looking inward, a raft of anatomy apps provides insight into the elegant construction and function of the human body. Many of these apps are designed for anatomy students or medical professionals and therefore may be more in depth than you'd need for casual anatomical study. The apps from Real Bodywork, a company specializing in massage-therapy training materials, strikes a good balance between being informative for a casual user without being overly technical. Their apps, Skeletal Anatomy 3d ($2.99), Anatomy 3d: Organs ($4.99), and Muscle & Bone Anatomy 3d ($6.99) are also a lot more affordable than the comprehensive apps designed for medical students. If you'd like to check out one of the med school–caliber apps, the Skeletal Head & Neck Pro III is a free app from a collection of anatomy apps designed with the Stanford University School of Medicine. Other apps in the series cost roughly $20.

To complete the trip from the vast reaches of space to the elemental building blocks of the universe, Nova Elements (free) is a beautifully designed app that makes chemistry fun. You can build your own atom, play the essential elements game and build atoms and molecules, or watch episodes of Nova's series *Hunting the Elements*. Together, they create an informative and entertaining experience that far exceeds the fun and educational value of the dry chemistry lectures I had in college.

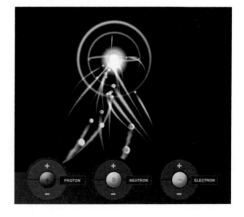

Build a Slender, Portable Reference Library

When I was young, my grandparents had a long shelf filled with volumes of the *Encyclopædia Britannica* (EB). Today, the app version of EB costs only $1.99/month and contains far more illustrations than its printed and bound predecessor. Links allow you to navigate between topics so you can follow your inquiries of discovery wherever they may lead.

I've already sung the praises of Wikipainion, one of five apps I consider "must-haves" for every iPad user. For your reference library, I would add the Dictionary app from Dictionary.com (free with ads; $4.99 ad-free), or for true lovers of language, the Oxford Deluxe dictionary ($54.99). Frequent users of the Wolfram|Alpha website for mathematical, data-driven search queries will find their mobile app ($3.99) to be a trustworthy companion.

Vicarious Museum Visits

Several top museums are bringing great design and important art to your iPad without your having to make a trip across town or across the country to catch the exhibit in person. Many of these iPad apps focus on a specific collection, like the America Folk Art Museum's Three Centuries of Red and White Quilts (free) or the Museum of Modern Art's Abstract Expressionist New York (free). I recommend the Design Museum app (free) to gain a deeper appreciation for industrial design, the American Museum of Natural History's Creatures of Light app (free) to learn about nature's self-illuminating species (see illustration), and the Getty Museum's interactive The Life of Art app (free), which uses the details in four pieces from their collection to teach about the history, function, and design of these beautiful items.

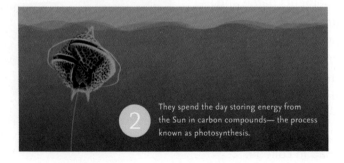

They spend the day storing energy from the Sun in carbon compounds— the process known as photosynthesis.

Three Bonus Apps to Kickstart Your iPad-Based Education

To help you begin your educational library, here are three apps that engage users with their interactivity, use of graphics and depth of information.

The Magic of Reality ($13.99)   This thought-provoking app from author Richard Dawkins and illustrator Dave McKean showcases the iPad's ability to explore the deepest questions that humans have puzzled over throughout our existence. The app uses mythology as a gateway into scientific inquiry and helps explain the mysteries of the universe, from who was the first person, to why we have night and day. Richly illustrated, the app uses text, video, and experiments disguised as games to lend a deeper appreciation for the plethora of scientific topics covered in this meaty book.

NASA Visualization Explorer (Free)   I've always had a fascination with astronomy, particularly the incomprehensible scale of galaxies and nebulae. To help make these concepts more concrete, the NASA Visualization Explorer app showcases the best images, videos, and stories gathered by NASA's scientists and fleet of satellites. Stories can be shared via Twitter, Facebook, SMS, or e-mail making it easy to spread the visuals you find awe-inspiring with your friends and social networks.

Khan Academy (Free)   Khan Academy is a nonprofit organization that uses video to teach a wide variety of subjects, from biology and geometry to computer science and American civics. The Khan Academy app is a portal to watch the 3,200 Khan Academy videos for self-paced and self-directed learning. Within the app, you can stream videos or download them to your iPad for offline viewing.

The iPad Lifestyle

People commonly think of the iPad as a productivity tool or a pathway to unending entertainment. While it is both these things and more, I encourage you to continue to explore new ways to use the iPad to enrich and organize your life. This section will show you how the iPad can be your most valued personal assistant, helping you stay in shape, find your way, shop and organize your finances, and hopefully give you an even better idea of the power of the iPad.

Stay Fit and Eat Well with Recipe, Diet, and Nutrition Apps

I love food and enjoy experimenting with new recipes. However, with the stresses of the daily grind, it can be easy to fall into a food rut and cook the same meals week in and week out. The recipe apps for my iPad spark my culinary creativity and encourage me to break out of the routine. Photos and videos do more to whet my appetite than a dry entry in a cookbook or magazine. Appetites (free) is one such app. Dishes are beautifully photographed, and short videos accompany each step of the creation process. This makes it easy to follow even advanced recipes. The free app includes a collection of recipes, and additional recipe packs can be purchased within the app to expand your recipe library.

Avocado Spring Rolls with Cilantro-Chili Dipping Sauce
by Gabi Moskowitz

A gorgeous appetizer that will impress your guests beyond belief.

Ingredients

10 8" rice paper spring roll wrappers

1 ripe avocado
1 ripe mango
1/4 head red cabbage
3 tbsp sweet chili sauce
1 small bunch cilantro
1 small piece ginger, peeled

Prep Time	Total Time	Yield
15 Mins	15 Mins	Makes 10 rolls

Less richly illustrated but more popular is Epicurious (free). You can search for recipes by ingredient and have the option to generate a shopping list from selected recipes and e-mail the list to your phone, or to your spouse, to make the trip to the grocery store quicker and easier.

Of course, with food and wine, it's easy to have too much of a good thing. That's where MyNetDiary ($9.99), a comprehensive, easy-to-use diet and calorie tracking app, can come in handy. You begin with your baseline height, weight, and target weight management goals and then, throughout the day, enter the food you eat. The database of more than 400,000 foods automatically adds the number of calories consumed. A separate exercise log allows you to track the calories you burn through exercise, and a Daily Details tab summarizes your progress, serves up kudos for what you've done well, and offers suggestions for improvement throughout the day. The app pairs with MyNetDiary's online service to enter and manage your data wherever you are, and an optional MyNetDiary Maximum service ($5/month) links your account to a Withings body scale or Fitbit for automated and more accurate weight and exercise tracking. With this service, you're also able to track cholesterol, blood pressure, blood glucose, and other essential metrics for managing your health.

Apps to Manage Your Finances and Prepare Taxes

Just as counting calories helps you lose weight, keeping a close eye on your finances helps you save money. Two apps in particular are outstanding for using your iPad as a dashboard to track your saving and spending habits. Mint.com, the popular personal-finance website, offers an outstanding companion iPad app (free). Mint.com links to your online bank account and credit card statements to give you an up-to-the-minute view of the money in your accounts and upcoming credit card bills. You can customize reminders to ensure you never forget to pay a bill on time, see your spending by category, set budgets, and even enter cash expenditures. This comprehensive app helps you track every penny you spend to help you make informed decisions about your personal finances.

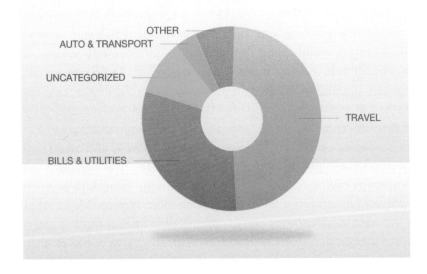

For business travelers, Expensify (free) is an app and web-based service that helps you collect and organize reimbursable expenses and then submit expense reports to your client or company. As someone who frequently has a wallet stuffed full of travel receipts that need to be submitted to clients, I appreciate the simplicity that Expensify brings to the process. Like Mint, Expensify is a comprehensive solution to collect the data you need for any type of reimbursable expense. Use the map to track mileage and calculate your mileage reimbursement. Snap photos of receipts and upload them to your Expensify account where they are scanned and matched to your credit card charges; then, when the job is complete, export your expense reports as a spreadsheet or bring it directly into Quickbooks to invoice your client.

To close out your financial year, you can use the H & R Block or TurboTax app (free; in-app charges to file tax return) to calculate your federal and state income taxes, tally up your deductions, and then file your taxes electronically. How well these apps will work for you largely depends on the complexity of your tax returns. If you have a simple tax return with few additional deductions or dependents, you'll find these apps to be convenient alternatives to other online tax preparation services. However, if you have several streams of income with large numbers of deductions, you may find the apps to be too limiting for your needs.

Reach Your Destination with Maps

The Maps app included with your iPad is a valuable copilot to help you figure out where you are, get to where you're going, and find the best route around traffic to minimize hassles along the way.

As one of the iPad's core apps, Maps is tightly integrated into the iOS operating system allowing it to be accessed as a stand-alone app or as a service from other apps. For example, Yelp, a restaurant review app, allows you to search for restaurants near your current location and then tap the one you like to get directions to the restaurant. For this, Yelp uses the built-in Maps and Location Services to identify your current location, then uses Maps again to direct you to the restaurant. In this way, Maps becomes an integral part of your iPad experience. Once you learn the basic features in Maps, your experience within any of the apps that use the Maps service becomes richer.

Find and Share Your Current Location

Have you ever wandered around an unfamiliar city and reached a point where you asked yourself, "Where on earth am I?" With your iPad and an Internet connection, you can quickly find your way. In order for this to work correctly, you'll need to have Location Services enabled (choose Settings | Location Services).

To begin, tap the Maps app icon to launch Maps, and then tap the Location Services icon at the top of the screen. This finds your current location on the map and marks it with a blue dot surrounded by a pale blue circle. The diameter of the circle indicates the estimated accuracy of the position on the map. The wider the circle, the less accurate the position indication will be.

Tap the blue dot marking your position to bring up information about your current location. Tap the orange-and-gray person icon to view your location in Google Street View (where available), or tap the blue-and-white "i" to bring up a Current Location pop-up menu.

This displays your current address and allows you to add the location to your contacts database; share your location via e-mail, Messages, or Twitter; or add the current location as a Maps bookmark. Like bookmarks in Safari, bookmarks in Maps help you remember a place. Within Maps, these are most commonly used as the starting or ending point for directions. For example, if you have a bookmark for your home and want to find directions from your home to a local sports arena, you can access the bookmark for your home and eliminate the need to retype your address.

Get Directions

Now that you know where you are, it's helpful to know where you want to go, along with the quickest way to get there. In the upper-left corner of the Maps window are two tabs to help connect you to the information you need: Search and Directions. Within the Search tab, enter a term, like **hardware store** or **espresso** in the Search field and tap Search on the onscreen keyboard. This performs a Google search and displays your results as red push pins on the map. Tap a pin to find more information about the location, or tap Directions To Here or Directions From Here to access directions between your current location and the selected location.

The Directions tab provides directions for driving, walking, or using public transportation to get between two points on the map. When you access the Direction heading, the Search field in the upper-right corner switches from a search bar to two location bars to enter the starting and ending points of your travels. Tap either field to open the onscreen keyboard as well as a pop-up menu displaying a list of recent destinations. As you type, Maps will attempt to match the address with information in your address book. This often makes it quicker to type the name of the person you're visiting instead of the address into the Location field. After you've entered the necessary information, tap Search on the onscreen keyboard to display directions to your destination.

 You can enter a search term like **espresso** in the directions field, and Maps will perform a search and display directions to the top search result.

The path to your destination is indicated with a blue line traveling from your starting point (green pin) to your ending point (red pin). A summary of your trip information is displayed on a slender blue bar at the bottom of the screen. The three icons at the left side of the bar allow you to choose between modes of transportation (driving, public

transportation, and walking). Along the
right side of the blue bar is the Start
button, which displays turn-by-turn
directions to reach your destination. Use
the arrow keys on the right side of the bar
to move through the list of turns. Alternate
routes may be shown in a lighter shade of
blue. To select an alternate route, tap the
route and the map will adjust accordingly.

When in Directions mode, you may also
notice that the lower-right corner of the
map curls slightly. This is a clue that hidden
features are waiting to be accessed with a
tap on the curled portion of the map. Here,
you can select between different types of maps, from satellite to
terrain; print your map; and, perhaps most importantly, display traffic
information on the map.

 Traffic information is not displayed on the terrain map.

With Traffic enabled, red areas indicate congested or slow-moving
traffic, while green means go—your route is clear. The traffic indication
can help you select alternate routes during rush hour or avoid
construction and unanticipated delays.

 At the time of this writing, Apple just announced an update to Maps
for the next version of your iPad's operating system. Details are not yet
available, but the new app, along with the rest of the iOS 6 software,
will be available in fall 2012.

So, there you have it, some handy, and in some cases, essential, apps
to make your life richer, easier, and run more smoothly. I encourage you
to keep exploring ways the iPad can be your companion to a life well
lived.

12

Dive Deeper into Your iPad

The third-generation iPad design, with the addition of Bluetooth 4.0, builds on the iPad's growing capabilities to link to a variety of commonly used devices and accessories, like printers, projectors, and wireless keyboards. Simultaneously, Wi-Fi, cellular, and Bluetooth connections enable app developers to rethink ways the iPad can be integrated into your daily life. As a result, an explosion of health-related apps and devices are being introduced to help iPad users track their weight, record their exercise routines, and even help people with diabetes monitor their insulin levels.

In the second half of this chapter, I'll show you how the iPad can help you keep in touch with your social networks, send text messages, and communicate in a foreign language.

Connect Your iPad to a World of Devices

As more people look to their iPad to replace their desktop or laptop computer, it becomes imperative for the iPad to work with commonly used computer devices, like printers and digital projectors. It isn't yet a perfect marriage, but as you'll see, your iPad is quickly becoming compatible with a number of devices and accessories.

Use Your Wi-Fi + Cellular iPad as a Wi-Fi Hotspot

If you have a Wi-Fi + Cellular iPad and are a Verizon subscriber, you can create a Wi-Fi hotspot from your cellular data connection.

1. In the Settings app, be sure Airplane Mode is disabled and your Cellular Data preference is set to On; then tap the Personal Hotspot heading to open the Personal Hotspot preferences window. If Bluetooth is not currently enabled, you'll see an alert asking if you'd like to enable Bluetooth on your iPad to share your connection over Bluetooth.

2. Swipe to turn the Personal Hotspot switch to "On" and enable the Personal Hotspot feature. When Personal Hotspot is active, you have three options for connecting to your iPad. The Personal Hotspot page provides step-by-step instructions for connecting, using each connection type.

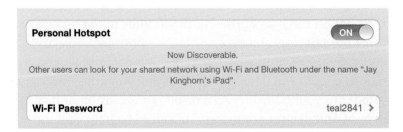

In my experience, Wi-Fi was the simplest to set up and most effective to use. The Bluetooth connection was by far the slowest of the three connection speeds, yet all three provided an Internet connection to my computer that was far slower than the connection speed measured on the iPad itself.

Print Documents from Your iPad

Despite the early promises of the Internet creating a "paperless office" there are still times that call for printed documents. Boarding passes, legal documents, and a printed copy of a book report to hand in for your homework are all still realities. To address this need, your iPad comes with AirPrint, a technology for wirelessly printing from your iPad to Wi-Fi-enabled printers, making it accessible to app developers to incorporate into their apps. Unfortunately, only a limited number of printers from Brother, Canon, Epson, HP, and Lexmark offer AirPrint support, significantly limiting the range of printers you can print to.

To see if your printer is AirPrint-enabled, visit http://support.apple.com/kb/ht4356 for a complete list.

If your printer is AirPrint-enabled, make sure your iPad and your printer are on the same wireless network. On your iPad, go to Settings | Wi-Fi to see which Wi-Fi network you're connected to. Follow the instructions provided with your printer to check the printer's Wi-Fi network status.

To print using AirPrint:

1. Tap the Action icon and then tap Print. (Note: This step may vary when working with non-Apple apps.)

2. In the Printer Options pop-up menu, tap the Printer heading and select your printer from the list of available printers. Use the + or – buttons to increase or decrease the number of copies of your document to be printed.

3. Tap Print.

If you don't have one of the supported models of printers, consider using Printopia 2 (Mac only, $19.95), an application that uses your computer as a print server to deliver files from your iPad to any printer via AirPlay. For Printopia 2 to work, your iPad and your computer need to be on the same wireless network. Printers can be connected via Universal Serial Bus (USB), Wi-Fi, or Ethernet. You'll need to first install the necessary print drivers and configure your computer to communicate with the connected printer. Once this step is completed, the printer will appear within your Print menu on your iPad.

Connect Your iPad to Your TV or Digital Projector

It's not practical to use the small screen of the iPad to watch a movie with your family, or to squish your colleagues together in a board meeting to show them the next quarter's financial statement. In situations like these, you need to connect your iPad to a TV screen or digital projector.

To do so, you have two options:

- Physically connect your iPad to the television using an accessory adapter and appropriate cables
- Wirelessly connect to supported devices with AirPlay

It's easy to connect your iPad to a projector or TV using either the Apple VGA or Apple Digital AV Adapter. Both attach to your iPad using the 30-pin connector at the base of the iPad and provide the necessary interface to connect with the corresponding cables for the TV or digital projector (HDMI for HD TVs or VGA for digital projectors and older TV sets). One difference to be aware of between the two types of connections: HDMI transmits sound and video while VGA is video only.

In both cases, your iPad's screen is mirrored and will appear on your TV or digital projector. The video feed supports up to 720p (standard HD) for movies and mirrored display up to 1080p (full HD).

AirPlay is a method for wirelessly delivering video or audio from your iPad to supported set-top TV boxes like Apple TV or Boxee or AirPlay-supported audio speakers. It is built into Apple apps like Music and Videos or apps from outside developers like Netflix, PBS, and TED.

To use AirPlay, first make sure your iPad and Apple TV (or other supported device) are connected to the same Wi-Fi network. Select the content you wish to display on your Apple TV then:

1. Tap the AirPlay button on the right side of the control bar in the Video app, or the upper-right corner in the Music app.
2. In the AirPlay menu, tap to select your Apple TV or other device from the list of available AirPlay devices.

When AirPlay is enabled, your iPad acts as a media server, streaming music, videos, Keynote presentations, or slideshows to your Apple TV.

To use the AirPlay controls:

1. Make sure the screen is illuminated and double-tap the Home button, or use the four-finger lift gesture to display the multitasking bar.

2. Swipe to scroll to the far left of the bar and tap the AirPlay icon.

In the AirPlay pop-up menu, tap the iPad heading to restore control to your iPad. If available, the Mirroring option allows you to mirror content between your iPad and your Apple TV.

The setup is similar in other apps like Netflix or PBS, though the location of the AirPlay button may differ based on the layout of the app.

Extend Your iPad's Utility with Accessories

An ecosystem of digital devices is growing rapidly to add functionality to the iPad. Withings Body Scale measures and records your weight, body composition, and body mass, and sends this information via Wi-Fi to a dashboard application on your iPad. The Square credit card reader transforms your iPad into a point-of-sale terminal for accepting credit cards. From cooking thermometers to iPad-controlled thermostats for your home, your iPad is quickly becoming the point of control for many devices in your life.

Connect to Devices with Bluetooth

Some of these devices that make your life easier and more flexible plug directly into the iPad using the 30-pin connector at its base. Others connect via Wi-Fi. An increasing number of devices use the Bluetooth 4.0 connection found in the third-generation iPad, which uses far less battery power than previous Bluetooth standards. Bluetooth is a technology for transmitting information over relatively short distances and is commonly used to connect mobile devices to headphones or earbuds, wireless keyboards, or external audio speakers. Bluetooth can also be used to connect your computer to your iPad and use your iPad's cellular data connection as a personal Wi-Fi hotspot.

To connect your iPad to a Bluetooth-enabled accessory:

1. Enable Bluetooth on your accessory to make it discoverable for your iPad.

2. In the Settings app, tap the General heading and then Bluetooth. Slide the Bluetooth switch to On.

3. When Bluetooth is enabled, a list of available Bluetooth devices is listed below the Devices heading.

If you're connecting to a device like a computer, you will be prompted to first pair the devices. For security purposes, a PIN code will appear in an alert on your iPad and on the computer's screen. Verify that the two numbers match, and then confirm the pairing on both the computer and your iPad.

To disconnect from a Bluetooth device, slide the Bluetooth switch to Off or tap the blue-and-white arrow to the right of the device's heading, and then tap Forget This Device. You will need to pair again with the device thee next time you wish to establish a Bluetooth connection.

It's a good idea to disable Bluetooth when you won't use it for an extended period of time to save battery power.

Travel the World with Your iPad

The next time you travel overseas be sure to pack your iPad along with your passport. Your iPad is a handy companion for researching travel destinations and accommodations, translating foreign languages, and making voice and video calls back home.

Prepare Your Wi-Fi + Cellular Model for International Travel

If you have a Wi-Fi + Cellular iPad, you'll want to take steps to make sure you don't return home to a large cellular data bill from your cellular provider. Your cellular data plan likely only covers your iPad's use within your home country. Use in other countries is billed at a much higher rate. The best way to avoid surprise charges is to disable the use of your cellular data connection outside your home territory. To disable data roaming:

1. Access the Settings app and tap the Cellular Data heading.

2. Ensure the Data Roaming switch is set to Off. (It is off by default.)

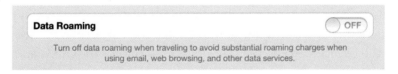

Swap Micro SIM Cards to Use International Carriers

If you plan to use a local cellular data carrier while overseas, you'll need to use the (Subscriber Identity Module) SIM eject tool that came with your iPad to remove the micro-SIM card that shipped with your iPad and insert one from your new carrier.

The SIM card is stored on the left side of your iPad opposite the volume switch. To remove and then reinstall a micro-SIM card on your iPad:

1. Insert the tip of the SIM eject tool into the small hole above the SIM tray slot. Press firmly and straight in until the tray pops out.

2. Pull out the SIM tray and remove the micro-SIM card.

3. Remove the SIM eject tool and insert the new card until it locks into place.

Before you leave for your trip, you'll want to research carriers in the country you're traveling to, see if they offer short-term or pay-as-you-go cellular plans, and confirm their service is compatible with your iPad. Apple provides several valuable tips for using cellular networks in other countries in this article found at http://support.apple.com/kb/HT1807.

Five Apps to Make Your Trip a Smooth One

Before you pack your suitcase, be sure to load up your iPad with these apps to help you explore your destination virtually, keep track of your reservations and keep in touch with friends, family (and even work) while you're away.

Google Earth   A great guide to preview your destination before you book your trip, Google Earth (free) provides a magic carpet for you to quickly fly over the terrain of any place in the world with stunning image quality and clarity. Be sure to enable the Panoramio Photos layer from the Layers menu to see user-generated photos of potential destinations.

Triposo   Another tool for researching potential trips, Triposo (free) collects and stores mini-guidebooks to countries around the world. Although the depth of the guidebook is not as great as those from

Lonely Planet, it is a valuable tool for research or for traveling between countries, as is often the case in Europe, where a slender informational guide and phrase book is all you'll need.

TripIt   After you book your reservations, TripIt (with ads, free; no ads, $3.99) will automatically scan your Inbox; aggregate the details for your trip; and create calendar events for your flights, hotel, transportation, and tours. Subscribe to your TripIt calendar feed and this information is added to Calendar on your iPad automatically.

Google Translate   *Você fala Português?* Do you speak Portuguese? No problem. Translate from Google (free) can help you communicate in foreign languages. An Internet connection is required for translation, which can be limiting in a crowded bazaar in Morocco, but in a café in Milan, you'll be just fine.

Skype   Place video and voice calls over Wi-Fi for free to other Skype users or make inexpensive international voice calls using this indispensable service. Our family uses Skype, which is free, to say hello when I travel; it allows my in-laws to watch our son grow up; and it helps us keep in touch with my brother-in-law's family in Dublin.

Safely Charge Your iPad's Battery Abroad

You'll want to check all your electronic devices to ensure you have the appropriate chargers and plug adapters for foreign electrical outlets. Your iPad's 10W power adapter indicates it is safe to use with international electrical currency standards between 100 and 240W. This means you're safe to use your iPad's power adapter to charge your iPad's battery from Japan (100v) to Kuwait (240v) and everything in between. You will, however, need a plug adapter to insert the power adapter into the wall. Apple sells the Apple World Adapter Kit ($39), which allows you to swap out the U.S. plug adapter with any of the world's standard configurations. You can also purchase a similar plug adapter from most travel stores.

Learn What's Coming Soon with iOS 6

The only constant about technology is change. As I write this final chapter in the book, Apple announced the next version of iOS, the operating system that runs your iPad. iOS 6 is expected to be released in fall 2012, and with it comes a host of new changes and improvements to make your iPad even more powerful, run more smoothly, and become more deeply integrated into your life. Because the software has not yet been officially released to the public, specific details are scant, but I do want to leave you with a high-level overview of the key features and changes you can expect when the software is released.

Siri The popular voice-activated personal assistant from the iPhone 4S, Siri, will be integrated into iOS 6 and will be available on the third-generation iPad. It is unclear whether or not this will replace the Dictation feature built into current iPads.

Maps The Maps app will be entirely new, with better, higher-resolution maps and spoken turn-by-turn navigation with real-time traffic updates. You'll be able to use Siri to control the Maps app, which will allow you to ask Siri to find an alternate route to your destination and avoid a traffic jam or to find restaurants and gas stations along the way.

Facebook Just as Twitter is integrated into Safari and other key apps on your iPad today, Facebook will be tightly integrated into the core functions of iOS 6. This will make it even easier to share content, photos, and location information with your Facebook friends.

FaceTime After many requests from the iPad community, FaceTime calls will be able to be made over cellular data networks. With any Internet connection (Wi-Fi or cellular), you'll be able to use FaceTime.

Photo Stream The Photo Stream service built into the Photos app is about to get a lot more powerful. In iOS 6, you'll be able to share your Photo Streams with select recipients. Your friends and family will be able to view and comment on them from supported Mac computers and iOS 6 devices, on the Web, or on Apple TV.

Safari   New integration with iCloud allows you to begin reading a webpage on one device and then finish the article from where you left off on another device—your open Safari tabs are stored in iCloud where they can be accessed by other iOS devices. Another great feature is the ability to store full webpages in your Reading list for offline reading.

 **How Will I Upgrade to iOS 6?**

If the features described have whet your appetite for iOS 6, stay tuned—lots more details will be made available closer to the release date. iOS 6 is expected to be a free upgrade for all supported iOS devices. When the software is officially released, you'll receive a badge notification in your Settings icon indicating that new software is available to download. Follow the directions in the appendix for upgrading your software, and you'll be ready to enjoy all the new features iOS 6 has to offer.

Appendix

Maintain and Troubleshoot Your iPad

Your iPad should give you years of trouble-free enjoyment. However, should problems arise, this section aims to help you resolve the most common problems iPad users encounter and will cover routine maintenance tasks like updating your iOS operating system.

Solving Problems

My experiences thus far with both a first-generation and a third-generation iPad have been free of troubles, barring the occasional app crashing. So if you're new to the iPad, don't let these troubleshooting tips alarm you; they are simply here in case you have a problem. Should you run into a problem that isn't covered in this section, check out Apple's iPad support pages at www.apple.com/support/ipad.

Force an App to Quit

Occasionally, an app gets stuck processing a task but doesn't crash. If this happens:

1. Double-tap the Home button or use the four-finger upward swipe gesture to display the multitasking bar.

2. Press and hold any of the apps until they begin to jiggle.

3. Tap the red-and-white circle icon on the left side of the app icon to exit out of the offending app.

Reset Apps or Your iPad

Worse than an app that freezes is an iPad that freezes or an app's alert dialog that crashes. You're unable to move to another application or exit out of the current app. You're stuck. There are two techniques to bring your unresponsive iPad back to life.

To force an app to quit when the technique listed previously doesn't work:

1. Press and hold the On/Off Sleep/Wake button for a few seconds until the red lock appears on screen.

2. Press and hold the Home button for several seconds to force the app to close. When completed, the red lock will disappear and you'll return to your Home screen.

A more comprehensive technique restarts your iPad entirely. This is a good remedy for resolving common problems. To restart your iPad:

1. Press and hold both the On/Off Sleep/Wake and Home buttons for at least ten seconds until the Apple logo appears on screen.

2. Allow your iPad to power off, and then press and hold the On/Off Sleep/Wake button to power up your iPad.

What to Do When Your Screen Won't Rotate

If your screen won't rotate, it is likely caused by one of two things:

- You have the rotation lock enabled.

- The app you're using doesn't support screen rotation.

If the rotation lock is enabled, you'll see the rotation lock icon in the status bar at the top of the screen. You can disable rotation lock in one of two ways depending upon whether you have the Use Side Switch To preference set to Lock Rotation or Mute.

- Double-tap the Home button to open the multitasking bar and swipe to scroll to the player controls at the far left of the bar. Tap the rotation lock icon to the left of the playback controls. If you see a volume icon instead of the rotation lock icon, proceed to option 2.
- Slide the Silent switch, located just above the volume rocker control, to release the rotation lock. However, there isn't anything you can do if an app doesn't support screen rotation.

Purge a Ghost App

A ghost app is an app that appears as a semi-transparent icon on your Home screen. Most often, ghost apps are caused by problems during the sync process. Unfortunately, you can't use the multitasking bar to make the app stop running or delete the app as you would normally. To get rid of a ghost app, you'll want to connect your iPad to your computer, launch iTunes, and perform the following steps.

1. Click your iPad's name in the Devices heading, and then click Apps.
2. Find the ghost app from the list of synced apps. Uncheck the box next to the app's name.
3. Sync your iPad to remove the app from your iPad.
4. When the sync completes, disconnect your iPad and tap the App Store icon.
5. Tap the Purchased heading, and then tap the Not On This iPad heading at the top of the screen.
6. Locate your ghost app from this list, and then tap the cloud icon to begin downloading and reinstalling your app.

My App Won't Download Completely

When you install apps using a less-than-reliable Wi-Fi connection, say in an airport or hotel, occasionally, the Wi-Fi connection drops while your download is in progress, causing your app to be stuck in a state of semi-installation. A partially downloaded app will show the installation progress bar and may show "Loading" or "Waiting" below the app icon, but the installation doesn't progress any further. To remedy your half-installed app issue:

1. Tap and hold the app icon on your Home screen until the icons jiggle.

2. Tap the black-and-white "X" to delete the app, and confirm your intent to delete the app in the resulting alert dialog.

3. Tap the Purchased heading, and then tap the Not On This iPad heading at the top of the screen.

4. Locate your app from this list, and then tap the cloud icon to begin downloading and reinstalling your app.

iPad Is Sluggish

If your iPad seems sluggish and less responsive, it may be time to close some open apps. You can do this in two different ways. The first option allows you to close apps manually through the multitasking bar. Press the Home button twice or use the four-finger upward swipe to open the multitasking bar. Tap and hold to make the app icons jiggle, and then tap the red-and-white icon in the upper-left corner of the app icon to close specific apps. When you're finished, tap the Home button.

The second method is to power off your iPad. Press and hold the On/Off Sleep/Wake button until the red lock appears on the screen. Slide the lock to power off your iPad. After a few moments, press and hold the On/Off Sleep/Wake button to power up your iPad.

Restore Your iPad from a Previous Backup

If your iPad is really causing problems and the techniques presented can't resolve the issue, your best bet is to restore your iPad's settings from a previous backup. You'll need to redownload any apps you've installed since the last backup. Follow the steps in "My App Won't Download Completely," once you've successfully restored from your backup. You can restore from either iCloud or iTunes on your computer, and you'll want to use the method you've been using for performing your routine backups.

To restore your iPad from an iCloud backup:

1. Erase your iPad by choosing Settings | General | Reset | Erase All Content And Settings. Confirm you wish to erase your iPad in the resulting alert.

2. Walk through the initial setup steps outlined in Chapter 1. At the sixth screen, titled "Set Up iPad," choose Restore From iCloud Backup.

3. On the next screen, you'll see the three most recent iCloud backups. Tap one that predates the problems you're experiencing.

4. After your iPad is restored, your apps, purchased content, books, and Camera Roll will begin downloading from iCloud.

You may be required to re-enter your passwords in your e-mail and other accounts to complete the restore process.

To restore your iPad from an iTunes backup:

1. In the iTunes window, click your iPad's name below the Devices heading.

2. On the Summary page, click Restore.

3. In the resulting dialog box, choose whether you'd prefer to back up the settings for your iPad before you restore the software. Apple recommends backing up your iPad and transferring all purchases before using the restore function.

4. In the next dialog, confirm you wish to restore your iPad to its factory settings and erase all content on your iPad.

5. After your iPad is returned to its factory settings, it will restart. Keep your iPad plugged in to your computer to begin the restoration process.

6. In the Set Up Your iPad window, select the backup iTunes should use for restoring your iPad from the pull-down menu.

The restoration process will take some time as your music library, apps, and other content are copied to your iPad. When the process is complete, disconnect your iPad from your computer.

What to Do When You Need Repairs

Problems happen. Perhaps your device wasn't assembled quite right at the factory or you spill coffee on your brilliant Multi-Touch screen. Regardless of the source of the problem, contacting Apple directly should be the first step in repairing your iPad. Your iPad's limited warranty covers hardware-related problems for up to one year from the date of purchase. AppleCare +, Apple's extended-warranty plan, covers up to two incidents of accidental damage, but the plan must be purchased within 30 days of the date of purchase.

If you're outside the warranty period or didn't purchase AppleCare + and have an "accidental damage incident"—for example, coffee on your iPad—your options are

- **Contact Apple directly** You can bring your iPad into an Apple retail store, or contact Apple Support to arrange for out-of-warranty service (OOW) or battery replacement. The OOW service swaps your current iPad with a model that is "new or equivalent to new" for $299. A battery replacement costs $99 plus $6.95 for shipping. More details on these services can be found at http://support.apple.com/kb/index?page=servicefaq&geo=United_States&product=ipad.

- **Have your iPad repaired by a third-party computer repair service** Unfortunately, Apple doesn't offer an Apple Authorized Service Center designation for iPads, though an Apple Authorized Service Centers designation for Macs can help guide you to a professional repair shop. Many service providers are able to replace a broken Multi-Touch screen, a common problem, less expensively than the OOW coverage from Apple. For example, a company I've used, MacWorks, Inc. (www.macworksinc.com/), charges $179.99 to replace the screen on a third-generation iPad.

It's always unfortunate when a problem arises. Fortunately, there are options to get your iPad back up and running without having to pay full price for a brand-new iPad.

Find My iPad

The Find My iPad service uses information from your iPad's Location Services and data from Wi-Fi connections to locate your iPad when it is lost, stolen, or misplaced. To use the Find My iPad locator, go to www .icloud.com and log in using the same Apple ID used to set up your iPad, or use the Find My iPhone app on your iPhone or a second iPad.

 For Find My iPad to work, Location Services must be enabled and the Find My iPad heading selected within Settings | Location Services. Your iPad's clock must also be set to accurately reflect the current time. This can be done by choosing Settings | General | Date And Time.

On the iCloud.com website, click Find My iPhone to bring up a list of your Apple devices. In the Find My iPhone app, tap the Devices heading in the top-left corner of the app to bring up a list of all your Apple devices. Click or tap your iPad in the devices list to search for your iPad's location. If your iPad is currently online, a map with your iPad's location will be displayed on screen. If not, a separate screen indicates the device is currently offline.

When you know your iPad is missing or stolen, the Find My iPad service gives you options for displaying your contact information on screen, locking your iPad, or erasing the contents of your iPad's hard drive remotely.

To activate these options from the iCloud website or the Find My iPhone app:

1. If your iPad is displayed on the map, click or tap the location pin on the map; then in the pop-up menu, click or tap the blue-and-white "i" to bring up the Information pop-up menu. If your iPad hasn't been located, you'll see three buttons on screen, identical to those found in the Information pop-up menu. If your iPad is not connected to a Wi-Fi network when you perform your search, you can instruct Apple to e-mail you when your iPad is located.

2. Click or tap Play Sound Or Send Message, Remote Lock, or
   Remote Wipe to activate any of these three options:

   - **Play Sound or Send Message**   Write a message to appear on
     your iPad's screen with or without an accompanying sound
     when the message is delivered.

   - **Remote Lock**   Remotely enables Passcode Lock on your iPad.
     Any user will have to enter the four-digit Passcode Lock code
     you enter on the website before they can use your iPad. If
     you suspect your iPad was stolen, engage the Remote Lock as
     quickly as possible. This renders your iPad useless (and less
     valuable) to a thief.

   - **Remote Wipe**   Erases the contents of your iPad. This is a
     last-ditch measure because when you erase your iPad you will
     no longer be able to locate it.

Find My iPad is a great tool for locating a lost, misplaced, or stolen
iPad. For even more protection against iPad theft, you may also
consider an app like GadgetTrak ($3.99), which allows you to take
pictures of the thief if your iPad is in use and e-mails them to you to
gather evidence for the police.

Update Your iPad's Software

Periodically, Apple releases updates to the iOS operating system, the
software that runs your iPad. When an update is available, you'll see a
badge notification on your Settings app and you'll see an indication
that new software is available when you sync your iPad through iTunes.
The update process is quick and straightforward, and your iPad will run
more smoothly and efficiently if you keep up with installation of all
available updates.

To update your iPad's software on your iPad:

1. Be sure to connect your iPad to your power adapter and plug
   the iPad into the wall. Should you run out of battery power
   while your operating system is in the midst of an upgrade, the
   results could be disastrous. You will also need an Internet
   connection to complete the upgrade process.

2. Tap Settings | General | Software Update. Available updates will be listed here. Typically, your iOS software update will download in the background while you use your iPad to make the update process faster. If it hasn't yet downloaded, tap the download button to download the update and prepare for installation.

3. Tap Install Now and then read and agree to Apple's Terms of Service document. Your screen will turn black and then the Apple logo will appear. A progress bar below the Apple logo indicates the installation's progress.

When the installation process is complete, your iPad will restart automatically and be ready to use with the new software.

To update your iPad's software using iTunes:

1. Verify you are using the latest version of iTunes. On Mac computers, select Check For Updates from the iTunes menu. On Windows, select Check For Updates from the Help menu.

2. Connect your iPad to your computer using the provided USB cable. In iTunes, click your iPad's name beneath the Devices heading.

3. On the Summary page, beneath the Version heading, you'll see a notice indicating a newer version of the iOS software is available to download and/or install. Click Update to begin the update process.

4. After the software update is downloaded to your computer, an alert will indicate the version of the iOS software you'll be updating to. Click Update.

5. The next dialog provides information on the improvements contained in the update. Click Next.

6. Read and agree to the software licensing agreement.

7. The screen on your iPad will turn black and then an Apple logo will appear. A progress bar below the Apple logo indicates the progress of the installation.

When the installation process is complete, your iPad will restart automatically and will be ready to use with the new software.

Now You Know **Transfer Purchased Apps and Content to iTunes**

When the time comes to update your iPad's operating system software, you may see a warning dialog indicating you have purchased content on your iPad that is not present in your iTunes library. To ensure all your content is transferred back to iTunes on your computer before moving forward with the update, go to the iTunes File menu and select Transfer Purchases From <Your iPad's Name>. This will direct iTunes to copy any new content not presently in your desktop iTunes library and protect against possible loss.

Back Up and Erase Your iPad Before You Sell It

Let's say the fourth-generation iPad has just reached store shelves and you're eager for an upgrade. Before you sell your third-generation iPad, you'll want to back up your settings from your current iPad to transfer your apps and settings to your new iPad. Then, you'll want to erase your third-generation iPad to get it ready for sale.

This is a two-part process that is easy to perform on your iPad.

1. Perform a backup of your iPad's software using whichever backup method you've been using regularly. To review the steps required to back up your iPad to iTunes or iCloud, please review Chapter 3.

2. When the backup is complete, open the Settings app on your iPad. Tap the General heading, and then tap Reset at the bottom of the screen.

3. Tap Erase All Content And Settings. In the Erase iPad alert, tap Erase to restore your iPad to factory defaults and remove all apps and personal data from your iPad.

4. Follow the instructions in the next section for removing your iPad from your list of devices associated with your Apple ID.

Remove Devices from Your Apple ID

When you set up your iPad for the first time, you entered your Apple ID, which associated your iPad with your Apple ID account. When you sell your iPad, you'll want to remove the iPad from your Apple ID account to make sure it doesn't count against your account's ten-device and computer limit.

To remove an iPad from your Apple ID:

1. Launch iTunes on your computer and, from the Store menu at the top of the screen, select View My Account.

2. Log in to your account; then from the Account Information page, click Manage Devices under the iTunes In The Cloud heading.

3. From the list of managed devices, locate the iPad (or other device) you wish to remove and click the Remove button.

An Apple device, like an iPad, can only be associated with a new Apple ID once every 90 days. This means that you can't purchase an iPad and then sell it 60 days later without the new owner being required to wait 30 additional days before they can enter their own Apple ID. If you've had your iPad for more than 90 days, you can sell your iPad and the new buyer will be able to enter their Apple ID and use the iPad normally without any additional delays or restrictions.

Index

S

Safari
- blocking pop-ups, 74
- bookmarks, 64–68
- clearing cookies, 73
- configuring preferences, 71
- copying images from webpages, 68
- creating shortcuts to a webpage on your Home screen, 69
- enabling/disabling JavaScript, 73
- finding specific text on a page, 70
- Fraud Warning, 73
- gestures and commands, 63–64
- in iOS 6, 233
- launching, 61
- online keyboard in, 61–63
- Private Browsing, 72–73
- Reader window, 64
- refining tabs and Bookmarks Bar, 72
- saving to Contacts, 70
- scrolling to top of page, 70
- sharing webpages via e-mail or Twitter, 69
- using AutoFill to fill out forms, 72
- using Dictation to browse, 71
- using tabs to view multiple pages, 68

screen. *See* Multi-Touch screen
searching, 30–31
- calendars, 105
- Reminders, 119

security
- Auto-Lock, 31–32
- cookies, 73
- Erase Data option, 33
- Find My iPad, 8, 241–242
- Passcode Lock, 31–33
- Private Browsing, 72–73
- Restrictions, 33–34
- Safari, 72–74
- *See also* locks

setup
- copying apps and settings from another iPad, 10–11
- iCloud, 8
- setup screens, 5–9
- using iTunes, 9–10

shaking, 12
Share And Print menu, 140
sharing files, 141
- transferring files using iTunes, 139–140

shortcuts
- creating, 35
- creating shortcuts to a webpage on your Home screen, 69
Silent/Screen rotation lock, 5, 35
SIM eject tool, 3, 229–230
Simple Passcode, 33
Siri, 232
Skeletal Anatomy 3d, 213
Skeletal Head & Neck Pro III, 213
Sketchbook Pro, 185
Skype, 203, 231
sleep mode, 4–5
SlideShark, 193
SlingPlayer, 145
sluggishness, 238
Smart Cover, 25
- iPad Cover Lock/Unlock, 34
Smart Playlists, 51–53
SMS messages. *See* Messages app
Snapseed, 183
social media, 145–146
- notifications, 203
- *See also* Twitter
SoundNote, 196, 197
Sounds tab, 29–30
- configuring sounds in Mail, 93
special characters, typing, 15
Spotify, 153–154
Spotlight Search, 30–31
Square, 197–198, 227
Story Patch, 208
streaming media, 153
Strip Designer, 210
styluses, 185–186
swiping, 12
- in Calendar's List view, 98
- four-finger swipe, 137
- in Safari, 64
symbols, typing, 15
syncing. *See* iCloud; iTunes

T

Tabletop, 188
tapping, 11
- in Safari, 63
- *See also* double-tapping
tech support, 235
TED, 133
television watching, 143–146
Terms and Conditions, 7